Finding My
Invincible Summer

MURIEL VASCONCELLOS

BALBOA.
PRESS

A DIVISION OF HAY HOUSE

ISBN: 978-1-4525-6179-0 (sc)
ISBN: 978-1-4525-6181-3 (hc)
ISBN: 978-1-4525-6180-6 (e)

Library of Congress Control Number: 2012920844

Balboa Press books may be ordered through booksellers or by contacting:
Balboa Press
A Division of Hay House
1663 Liberty Drive
Bloomington, IN 47403
www.balboapress.com
1-(877) 407-4847

This book is a work of nonfiction. Unless otherwise noted, the author and the publisher make no explicit guarantees as to the accuracy of the information contained in this book and in some cases, names of people and places have been altered to protect their privacy.

Because of the dynamic nature of the Internet, any web addresses or links contained in this book may have changed since publication and may no longer be valid. The views expressed in this work are solely those of the author and do not necessarily reflect the views of the publisher, and the publisher hereby disclaims any responsibility for them.

The author of this book does not dispense medical advice or prescribe the use of any technique as a form of treatment for physical, emotional, or medical problems without the advice of a physician, either directly or indirectly. The intent of the author is only to offer information of a general nature to help you in your quest for emotional and spiritual well-being. In the event you use any of the information in this book for yourself, which is your constitutional right, the author and the publisher assume no responsibility for your actions.

Printed in the United States of America

Balboa Press rev. date: 11/09/2012

To Sylvio

In the depth of winter
I finally learned
there was inside me
an invincible summer.

—Albert Camus

Contents

Acknowledgments

We write to expose the unexposed. If there is one door in the castle you have been told not to go through, you must. Otherwise you'll just be rearranging furniture in rooms you've already been in. Most human beings are dedicated to keeping that one door shut. But the writer's job is to see what's behind it, to see the bleak unspeakable stuff, and to turn the unspeakable into words.
—Anne Lamott

My editor, Carolyn Allen, led me to understand that this book is about opening doors that I would have preferred to leave closed and exploring places where I didn't want to go. She encouraged me to write about the unspeakable. While rarely suggesting her own wording, Carolyn consistently helped me to find the real story underneath the public face. Thanks to her, I learned that I could speak in ways that have surprised me. I discovered the power of opening those doors and found a voice that I didn't know I had. Without her patience and wise advice at every turn, the outcome would have been entirely different. I am grateful to her beyond measure.

I also want to express deep gratitude to Amy Duncan for reading the manuscript twice and giving me many excellent suggestions. In addition, I am very grateful to my proofreaders, Mariah Braxton and Sandy Gough.

Part I

Round One

———

1

ON A WARM FALL DAY in 2001, I sat on the front stoop of a small hotel in one of Washington's older tree-shaded neighborhoods, waiting for Dr. Laird to arrive. Dr. Thomas Laird was the surgeon who first told me I had breast cancer back in 1977. He was also the one who concluded three years later that the cancer had spread to my bones and predicted I had less than six months to live. A mutual friend thought it was time for us to meet again, so here I was, more than twenty years after his prognosis.

When he arrived, Dr. Laird greeted me with a warm smile and an outstretched hand. Without any preamble, the first thing he said was:

"It's times like these, I'm happy to be wrong!"

My cancer crisis happened a long time ago, and I have outlived many of the characters in the story. What makes my experience somewhat different is that I ultimately walked away from treatment when doctors were telling me I would not survive if I did. As I learned gentle approaches to becoming physically and emotionally healthy, cancer became a non-issue. I haven't seen an oncologist since 1983, and as far as I know, I am cancer-free.

My episodes with cancer were intertwined with the story of loving and losing my husband Sylvio. His support made everything possible; his death shattered me to the core. In my vulnerable state, I struggled to deal with grief, guilt, and eventually, when I was told that my cancer had spread, helplessness and hopelessness. Then one day I had an experience that shifted my perspective, and glimpses of a bright new world opened up to me.

As I began to move beyond the limiting beliefs I had held for most of my life, new insights constantly expanded my awareness and understanding. They always seemed to appear at the moment I was ready for them.

While I wouldn't wish cancer on anyone, for me it was the catalyst that changed everything. As I write these lines, it's hard for me to recognize the person I was three decades ago. My journey led me to freedom, power, and, ultimately, deep inner peace—my invincible summer.

I discovered my lump on April Fools' Day, 1976. I woke up early that morning, and as I stretched my arms, my fingers brushed against a hard knot on the inside of my right breast next to the bone. It was large, round, solid, and different. I felt it again, to make sure it wasn't my imagination. And again. With each pass of my fingers, I came closer to the certainty that it was cancer. My thoughts began to spin into full gear. As I lay there, I worked myself into a high state of anxiety.

With no doubt in my mind, I was already processing the diagnosis. I was going to die, and I was only 42! People aren't supposed to die so young. I couldn't believe that this was happening to *me*. Cancer was for other people, that minority of—what was the ratio?—one in four? I didn't know the statistics, but I was sure that many more people don't get cancer than do. Not only was it cruelly unfair, it was unreal. I had been normal the night before, and now I was staring at death.

At the time, my life was going really well, after decades of struggle. I had met my husband six years earlier, and I was more in love with him than ever. Challenges had claimed our attention earlier, but now we were finally able to relax. We had come to a happy place, and we had earned it.

We lived in a charming little rowhouse on Corcoran Street near Dupont Circle, not far from everything the Nation's Capital had to offer. The narrow street, lined with towering gingko trees that turned yellow in autumn, was a quiet oasis surrounded by busy avenues. I had bought the house shortly before I met him, at a time when property values were low. It was a tiny jewel, perfect in every detail, and I furnished it lovingly. Few things have given me more pleasure in life than fixing up my homes, starting with an elaborate Victorian dollhouse that was my hobby for many years. The Corcoran Street place was my grown-up dollhouse.

I had a job that I enjoyed. For the past year I had been in charge of producing a quarterly journal in the field of public health. I got to plan the content, draft short features and abstracts, ghost-write articles, edit, translate, and play with layout and design. Plus, the journal had a mission; it was making a difference. The job was a good fit for me. The only downside was occasional tension with my boss over "artistic differences."

Besides the job, I was doing freelance translation in my spare time, and I was also teaching translation at Georgetown University. I enjoyed that work the most.

I was the happiest I had ever been, but now I suddenly saw myself losing it all to cancer.

I decided not to tell Sylvio about my discovery. I didn't want him to worry until I had something concrete to report.

The lump that was so obvious to me turned out to be less obvious to the professionals. My gynecologist dismissed it and told me I simply had "lumpy breasts." He did consent to ordering a mammogram, and to my surprise, the films showed nothing:

> The clinically palpable nodule described on the right in the upper quadrant apparently blends in with . . . zones of dysplasia. **No X-ray criteria of neoplasm can be identified** on either side in either projection.

In other words, the lump had not shown up at all.[1] It was there, but it was on the opposite side of the breast from the camera. Looking back, I realize that the procedure itself was quite clumsy by today's standards: the technician positioned my body on a large table with my arms and legs splayed out at odd angles, then slid the film directly underneath my breasts, never applying compression. Later I looked at the films myself and thought I could see a shadow, but that was through the lens of hindsight.

Based on the report, my gynecologist said there was no possibility that I had cancer. Again: I simply had "lumpy breasts." I didn't believe him, and my anxiety kept mounting. After a while, I consulted another doctor and tried to get him to request a second mammogram. He told me it was "too soon." Apparently it didn't occur to him that the first one could have been flawed or that a second one might have yielded a better picture.

Even back then, the public was bombarded with the message that early detection is crucial. Yet it wasn't happening. As months went by, I felt increasingly betrayed—by the doctors who dismissed my concerns, and by a technology and a system that didn't work. The way I saw it, mammography was defective because it didn't show the image of my lump, and the system was broken because my life was depending on one person's interpretation of a set of photos. My resentment and frustration were immense, and they festered. I fed them continuously with a taped message in my head that kept repeating:

"I've got cancer and no one cares!"

In the summer I began to have shooting pains in my arm, which added to my distress. They would start near the lump, cross over to the right shoulder, and go down my arm into the palm of my hand.

I saw the gynecologist again, and he reiterated his position.

Often I would wake up at night and cry in the dark, partly from the pain, but mostly from the belief that my life was slipping away and no one was going to rescue me.

My job situation took a turn for the worse. I began to have regular clashes with my boss. While editing was the first professional opportunity that had opened up for me, in my heart I had wanted to be a translator more than anything else. My passion for translation dated back to eighth grade, when I started to learn Spanish. I had been doing freelance translating on the side for more than 15 years. I like translation because it gives ideas a wider audience. This is especially true for English, the international language of science. Translation nourishes my desire to make a difference in the world. It's also my art form: I feel that I'm painting with words.

Over the summer, two different job openings materialized, both of them positions for a full-time translator and both a step up the ladder career- and money-wise. The first was in my own organization. I took the test, and I thought I did well, but I didn't get the job. It went to someone from the outside. Since it was the office's only post for a translator into English, missing out on it was a huge disappointment. It seemed terribly unfair. I felt more frustrated than ever. The other opportunity came up a couple of months later at a sister organization. The salary was higher, the work was interesting, and I was excited about the prospect of a change. I took a day-long test in September together with a large group of other translators.

All the while, my lump was getting bigger. In November a discharge started to seep from the nipple. When that appeared, once again I made an appointment to see the gynecologist. He was getting really impatient with me. He told me point blank:

"As I said before, you just have lumpy breasts. You won't find a conscientious surgeon who would biopsy that."

In mid-December I received the call I had been waiting for: I was selected for the new job! My heart did cartwheels. I was beyond joy. Only briefly did I stop to wonder how I could have been rejected by my own organization, yet come out the winner in a much larger field of candidates and in an area that wasn't my specialty.

But there wasn't time for rumination. That same afternoon I went in to sign papers and schedule appointments, one of which was a routine medical exam.

A week later, the insurance doctor took one look at the lump and requested a biopsy. My nine-month wait was finally over.

2

THOUGH GETTING A DIAGNOSIS HAD been my top priority, my search for answers was not matched by a desire for invasive treatment. I wanted a surgeon who would not be aggressive. I started asking around, and before long I was referred to Dr. Laird.

I waited through the holidays. I still hadn't told Sylvio about the lump because I didn't want to spoil Christmas. I broke the news to him the day after New Year's, just before I called to make an appointment. Naturally, he was concerned. Dr. Laird saw me the next day. The first thing he did was try to aspirate the lump to see if it contained fluid, which would indicate that it was probably a benign cyst. There was no fluid. The lump was solid. I wondered why no one had done that before.

"Lumps don't belong in the breast," he said. "We'll have to do a biopsy."

Still, I made it clear to him that I didn't want my whole breast removed. That was very important. I explained that I had inherited a distrust of the mastectomy from my grandparents—he, a surgeon, and she, a breast cancer survivor who was cured with radiation alone in 1940, when the technology was in its infancy.

I had been aware of the growing movement against radical mastectomy long before my own lump appeared. This was a topic that was often discussed in my family. I knew my grandfather believed that cutting out a tumor contributed to the spread of cancer—the more extensive the surgery, the greater the spread.

Grandfather was influenced by his friend and colleague, George Crile, Sr., founder of the Cleveland Clinic, who was one of the first to publicly raise questions about the radical mastectomy. His son, George Crile, Jr., went on to promote the *lumpectomy*—in other words, a biopsy with removal of the surrounding tissue— and showed that it was just as effective, without the complications. I had read his book on the subject,[2] and was aware that he had devoted his career to fighting unneeded surgery and what he called "the battle of the breast."[3]

When my time came, I realized that, despite the efforts of the Criles, their views were not yet widely accepted. In fact, when I was facing my biopsy in January 1977, the invasive mastectomy was still the standard of care. Women were hospitalized, and the breast biopsy was done under general anesthesia. If tissue from the tumor was found to be cancerous, the next step was to remove the breast, as well as some or all of the lymph nodes under the arm, while the patient was still on the table. It was the way things were done, and few people asked questions. Most surgeons believed that doing anything less was irresponsible.

If I hadn't found Dr. Laird, I would probably have had to go under the knife not knowing if I was going to wake up permanently maimed on one side of my chest. Reconstruction, if I had wanted it, was rarely done and prohibitively expensive. Most insurance plans didn't cover it.

All that has changed, thanks in large part to the activism of author and journalist Rose Kushner.[4] At the time I was facing my biopsy, she was about to begin her tireless campaign against one-step surgery so that women could have a voice in their treatment and be offered more options, including lumpectomy. The scenarios that she advocated, and that George Crile, Jr., had been struggling to get accepted since the 1950s, are now the norm. Even so, that hasn't stopped surgeons from performing invasive mastectomies, and some experts claim that as many as half the mastectomies being done today are unnecessary.[5]

I asked Dr. Laird for what Rose Kushner called the "two-step procedure"—in other words, I wanted him to wake me up after the biopsy. Besides not trusting extensive surgery, I believed that radiation was the better alternative. In 1940, my grandmother refused surgery for breast cancer and insisted on radiation instead, even though the technology was still very new. She lived another twenty years and died of other causes. My lump was on the same side as hers, and I wanted to follow her example—or at least minimize the surgery.

Dr. Laird scheduled the biopsy for January 10, and he promised to wake me up before he did anything else.

While I trusted his word, I wasn't taking any chances. When I checked into the hospital the night before, I refused to sign a routine authorization allowing the surgeon to proceed with a mastectomy if the biopsy was positive. That created quite a stir with the hospital staff. It was the first of many times I would take a stand against the system.

Back from surgery the next morning, from the window of my hospital room I could see bright sunshine glinting on a chill landscape of snow and ice. Wind rattled the windows and pushed against the trees. The streets were sheer glass, too treacherous for driving. My normally late-rising husband, an import from the warm tropics of Brazil, had gotten up at five o'clock in the morning, braced himself against the alien cold, and made his way across the city on a bus.

We were alone. It was a secret that I was in the hospital; family and friends had not been told. We waited numbly for Dr. Laird to come and report the results of the biopsy. To pass the time, we played *Biriba*, a Brazilian card game. Our hearts weren't in it, but it kept us busy. He was very clever at cards, so I usually lost. This time he was letting me win. He pretended to be baffled by my winning streak.

"*Outra vez!*"—Not again!

It was his little gift to me, his effort to cheer me up.

My right breast was wrapped in thick bandages, and I couldn't feel a thing. I was still under the effects of general anesthesia. My thoughts were skating in circles somewhere outside my head.

Dr. Laird finally appeared. He had been waiting for the final lab results. Yes, he said, there was a tumor: an invasive ductal carcinoma about an inch in diameter—2.5 centimeters to be exact.

So it *was* cancer! Just as I had expected. While I was alert enough to feel vindicated, my brain was too numb to fully absorb the news and all that it implied.

Dr. Laird went on to say that the particular type of tumor was not very aggressive and he had been able to remove all of it, as far as he could tell. Even so, he said that more tissue had to be taken from around the site. I went along with the discussion about what to do next. I was in no condition to engage in debate. Moreover, I was in uncharted territory.

We reviewed the options, from a conservative to a radical mastectomy. "Lumpectomy" was off the table; Dr. Laird said it would not be sufficient. Sylvio, with his Cartesian mindset, thought "radical" sounded safer. He also suggested removing the other breast as well, pointing out that Happy Rockefeller, the Vice President's wife, had recently had her second breast removed as a precaution. He wanted everything possible to be done. While I was more interested in minimizing the surgery, I knew that he meant well, and it was reassuring that he wanted *me*, even without breasts.

We finally agreed on a *partial* mastectomy: about one-third of the breast would be removed. Dr. Laird explained that this procedure was more extensive than a lumpectomy, but he assured me that I would still be able to wear "revealing gowns."

No lymph nodes would be taken from under the arm. That was important to me, because I believed it was serious surgery that could lead to complications, including spread of the disease. Dr. Laird felt that it was a safe decision. To satisfy Sylvio's concerns, core needle biopsies would be taken from the other breast, entering through the nipple. Reconstruction was not discussed, nor would my insurance have paid for it. When it became available a number of years later, I was reluctant to do the surgery. I remain somewhat deformed.

While chemo wasn't mentioned, follow-up radiation was scheduled as part of my treatment. That was fine with me. Remembering my grandmother, I believed it was the right thing to do. As Dr. Laird put it:

"Like wearing a belt and suspenders at the same time."

I didn't know it at the time, but the metaphor was common. A decade later, Saturday Night Live comedian Gilda Radner appeared on the cover of *Life* magazine wearing a belt and suspenders.[6] Though she had initially resisted radiation, she made peace with it and was proudly showing off her suspenders, a symbol of the added treatment that she believed had helped to save her life.[7] For me, too, the idea was comforting at the time, and I trusted the plan.

I began to feel greatly relieved. Not only was the tumor under control, but my long months of frustration and fear were over. Also, I have to admit, I felt a certain satisfaction in knowing I had been "right"! It was validation, my unspoken "I told you so" to the gynecologist and others who had been so dismissive. I felt reassured that my perceptions had been accurate—that I wasn't the "hysterical female" that my gynecologist seemed to think I was.

It was not the first time that my voice had been disregarded. I had a long history of not being heard or understood, and it has always been one of my deepest frustrations. If I feel unheard or disbelieved, I tend to become very intense. During the nine months that I was insisting I had cancer, my rising desperation may well have worked against me as I tried to get people to listen.

The next morning I was rolled back to the Operating Room for the partial mastectomy. Three days later I went home. The pain was gone from my arm and hand, and for a while I felt content. My problem was solved. When I saw Dr. Laird, he reassured me that we had caught the cancer in time. Now I could get on with the business of living and start my new job.

Unfortunately, this sense of relief didn't last very long. About a week after my surgery, a letter arrived in the mail from my prospective employer. I was certain it was confirmation of my appointment, and I opened it excitedly. As I read the lines, my heart sank. They couldn't hire me. Citing my diagnosis and surgery, they explained that their health insurance could not cover any future cancer-related expenses. I was stunned. At no point had it crossed my mind that I was not going to get the job. By "taking care" of the cancer, I believed that my slate would be clean and recruitment would proceed. Frantic, I called the personnel office and the nurse to explain that my cancer was different. It wasn't going to come back. I promised that there would be no more medical expenses. I even volunteered to pay for any future costs from my own pocket. But they wouldn't budge. The decision had been made.

I was inconsolable. I sobbed all night long. Sylvio stayed up and tried to comfort me.

I was struggling with this disappointment, as well as severe bronchitis, when I checked in for six weeks of daily cobalt-60 radiation in the third week of January—the "suspenders" part of the agreement. The radiation oncologist informed me that both the tumor site and the lymph nodes were going to be targeted. I would be getting a heavier dose because I had not had a full mastectomy and the lymph nodes were still intact.

"Any questions?" he asked.

I did have questions. First, radiating the lymph nodes didn't make sense to me. In my work as a medical editor, I had come to understand that they play an important role in combating disease. Even more worrisome, I wanted to know if healthy cells were going to be killed along with the malignant ones. While I understood that the idea was to stop any spread of cancer in the area around the tumor, sacrificing healthy cells in the process seemed unwise. The doctor explained, almost condescendingly:

"The cobalt rays are smart enough to scavenge for malignant cells and leave the healthy ones alone. And if the healthy ones should happen to get damaged, they can repair themselves."

I tried to believe him, but I wasn't convinced.

At my next visit, his people took measurements, poked me a lot, and whispered to each other. They used a marker to trace thick black lines across my chest and back. I was told I had to protect the lines when I bathed so that they wouldn't wear off, and I felt grimier and greasier as the weeks wore on.

In fact, each visit to Radiation Oncology—buried deep in the hospital basement—was more uncomfortable than the one before. I felt dwarfed and dehumanized by the mammoth bulk of the machines. The patients were products on an assembly line, passed from station to station. As we came in, the head nurse, a former army officer, would order us to "Suit up!" Then we would sit waiting on a bench in a row, shivering in our flimsy hospital gowns.

Each day, I was cooked on both sides like a hamburger. As the treatments progressed, my skin got raw and itchy from the high-necked tops I was wearing to cover up the black lines. I felt more and more out of sorts. Sometimes I was nauseated, and always I coughed. My chest condition was getting progressively worse. I was also swallowing a lot of air, and I had constant indigestion.

Whenever I told the doctor about symptoms I was having, he would quickly attribute them to something besides the radiation. He ordered a variety of tests, including a barium X-ray to make sure I didn't have an ulcer. By the fourth week I had developed oozing blisters over an area that coincided exactly with the radiation fields on my front chest.

"It's probably the soap you're using," he said.

He always had an answer. The treatment was not to be questioned.

I later learned that the World Health Organization recognizes "moist exudation" as an undesirable side effect of radiation therapy, level 6 on a scale of 0 to 9.[8]

If I had misgivings, Sylvio echoed them tenfold. He wanted me to stop. I didn't think that was an option. I believed that the treatment was important to my survival, so that I could get on with life. And I remembered my grandmother. So I kept going, making my way along streets and sidewalks packed with snow and ice, which turned into slush as the weeks wore on.

The radiation oncologist was a committed man—a five-star general in the war on cancer. I was about halfway through my treatment when one day I was reading the newspaper and my eye fell on an article titled "Atom Smasher Is Newest Weapon in Tumor War." As I read on, I realized that my own doctor was being interviewed about experiments he was conducting in his spare time using a government atom smasher. The two-block-long machine was owned by the U.S. Navy and valued at many millions of dollars. This behemoth was being aimed at tumors in dogs and human volunteers.

"Regular radiation," he explained to the reporter, "is like shooting at cells with a single-shot rifle. The neutron beam is like using a machine gun."

I began to visualize myself at the business end of this colossal weapon, the target of his primal wrath.

Between my blisters and the story about the atom smasher, Sylvio wanted me to stop more than ever. We argued; he got sullen. I persisted doggedly for the entire six weeks, never missing a day. Looking back, I understand that fear for my survival was shutting out any thoughts about the wisdom of the treatment. I had tricked my mind into accepting almost everything I was told during my daily visits to Radiation Oncology. I lost touch with my inner questioning and common sense.

At the end, the doctor reported for the record that I had received a total of 4,800 radiation absorbed doses (rads) to the breast (with a soaked pad over the surgical scar to intensify the effect); 4,600 rads to lymph nodes in several places; and 1,200 to a booster field on the back. I don't know if that's an unusual amount, but roughly speaking, it was the radiation equivalent of 150,000 to 350,000 chest X-rays today. The lymph nodes in my right armpit and under the breastbone, which I believed were so essential to health, were fried to a crisp in a deliberate effort to destroy them.

Part II

A Love Story

3

M Y EXPERIENCE WITH CANCER IS part of a much larger tapestry of interwoven threads. At the heart and center of this tapestry was a beautiful love story. Until I met Sylvio, my life had been turbulent for as long as I could remember. With him, I felt secure, supported, and fulfilled. He became my anchor as we faced our challenges together. The story of our love began seven years before my partial mastectomy.

When we met, I was 36 and Sylvio was 53. Though we would become equal partners, in some ways he filled the role of the father I never really had. He was also my brother-in-law. My first husband was his younger brother John, a psychiatrist who practiced in Maryland and had died from a brain aneurism the year before at the age of 45. John and I had only been married briefly. He had told me about his brother Sylvio, but I had never met him. I had never even seen a photograph.

Sylvio and John were born in Belo Horizonte, Brazil. While John migrated to the United States, Sylvio remained there and became dean of the university's School of Architecture and also held a job protecting colonial cities in the state of Minas Gerais— including Ouro Preto, a UNESCO World Heritage site.

He showed up in my life quite unexpectedly. He was carrying some serious baggage. As I already knew, he had been imprisoned by the Brazilian military in 1965. Everyone was shocked that a distinguished university professor with no political agenda would be a target of revenge by the military dictatorship. In fact,

Sylvio never did understand why he had been singled out for punishment. It was a Kafkian situation that outraged his family and friends and bent his spirit almost to the breaking point.

It could be that he had rubbed a few too many people the wrong way in his zeal to safeguard national heritage, doing what he believed was right. He had squared off against developers more than once, even taking powerful stakeholders to court to stop them from tearing down colonial treasures. Around the time the military dictatorship came to power, he won a court case in which a colonial church was spared the wrecking ball. The court's decision put a halt to plans for a large urban development project.

His ordeal began a few months later. He was at home reading the newspaper one evening when armed men in uniform showed up at his door. They took him away. Terrified and dismayed, he thought it had to be a mistake. He had never espoused political causes. He couldn't possibly imagine what they wanted him for.

At first he was kept in a crowded holding cell, and then he was transferred to a military prison, where he remained for a number of months. In the meantime, family and friends were working to get him released, and eventually they succeeded. However, he still didn't know the "crimes" he had been charged with. When the charges were finally revealed years later, they were preposterous and irrelevant. His logical mind could never face the irrational insanity of what happened to him, and eventually he became too embittered to even consider an explanation.

By the time he was released, the military in power had "retired" him prematurely from both of his jobs and granted him a small pension, effectively preventing him from continuing the work he had been doing and leaving him unemployed.

He felt he had no choice but to leave the country "for the duration." It was the beginning of a four-year odyssey that took him to Portugal, then France, then Chile, and then back to Brazil. Just when he thought he could breathe a sigh of relief, he learned that a new order had been issued to send him back to prison.

He had to leave again, and he started looking for somewhere to go. His first opportunity was a cultural mission in the United States, at the invitation from the U.S. State Department, and that is how he ended up in Washington, D.C., on a chilly morning in April 1970.

He was in Washington for meetings and interviews before he started out to visit cities around the country. I had no idea he was coming. In fact, I had never had any contact with him whatsoever. I was sitting at my desk in my office when his call came. He took me totally by surprise. We arranged to meet for lunch. As it happened, he was staying at the Dupont Plaza Hotel, a block from my home on Corcoran Street.

I went to his hotel, and our eyes first met as he stepped out of the elevator. He stood a shade under 6-foot-4 and was the handsomest man I had ever seen. He looked like a Latino version of the Arrow shirt man: slim, with dark wavy hair and perfect features. Not only that, he had big, strong, beautiful hands and a deep bass voice. I caught my breath and thanked myself for the years I had spent studying Portuguese.

Although he understood written English perfectly, he could not carry on a conversation. He had been assigned an interpreter to escort him during his scheduled program, but there were other things he wanted to do, and I was more than happy to take time off from work and accompany him in between his official appointments.

I particularly remember one cold morning when I met him halfway as he walked toward my house. He was wearing a long vicuña scarf with one end trailing behind him. What a dramatic figure he was! My heart skipped several beats. That was the moment when I knew I had feelings for him. I tried to ignore them, because, of course, he was my brother-in-law. And I knew nothing about his personal life.

Over the days that followed, I became completely entranced by how easily and articulately Sylvio could talk about any subject, using wry humor to make his point. His nephew Márcio, who was living in Baltimore, came down to see him, and as I followed the threads of their exchange, I found myself wishing the evening would never end, or that I could belong to their world and listen to them forever.

Shortly afterwards, Sylvio and I had a conversation that took our relationship to a more personal level. It turned out that we had both suffered deep emotional wounding from being tall. As we opened up and talked about it, we became very close. We realized that we shared feelings that few people could understand. It wasn't just the fact of being tall; it was the history that went with it.

He told me about being teased as a child, and the bad dreams he still had about his height. He believed that it made people uncomfortable and envious, especially in Brazil where the difference was more noticeable. He sensed that they would unconsciously try to gain stature or even the playing field by saying and doing subtle things that hurt. More than anything, he yearned to blend in and look like everyone else.

I understood so well. I told him how I towered over the other kids in elementary school. They would line up on the playground during recess and chant: "Muriel is B-I-G! Muriel's a P-I-G!" In seventh grade gym class, a girl said to me: "You have no idea how ridiculous you look!" The wounds remained with me even as an adult. People never understood if I told them how I felt. No one tried to put themselves in my shoes and experience my hurt—until Sylvio.

I told him all this. We knew instantly that we were kindred souls. We were both misfits. We now had a bond.

During his three-week tour around the country, he phoned me several times and sent me notes and post cards. By the time he returned to Washington on May 4, the weather was hot. It was the day before my birthday, and he asked his interpreter to help him buy me a gift. He decided on an ounce of Chanel N⁰ 5⁹ surrounded by a bouquet of pink roses. The interpreter disapproved:

"That's too much," he said. "You hardly know her. We don't do things like that here."

But Sylvio had plans. He proposed to me on my birthday. He had applied for a two-year job in Mexico City with the Organization of American States, and he asked me to go with him if the job came through. I was stunned. We had never held hands, let alone kissed. We had been together only ten days, not counting the time he was traveling. I still knew nothing about his personal life.

I was as bewildered as I was swept away. I asked him about his family, and he told me what I needed to know. I listened to my heart, and without hesitation I said "yes." It was by far the best decision I ever made.

4

WHILE MARRYING AN AMERICAN MAY have been expedient, Sylvio later claimed that getting a U.S. visa had never been his motivation. His intention, when he first looked me up, had been to offer me assistance in handling his brother's affairs. He believed he had enough resources to manage on—including a research grant in Portugal and a Guggenheim fellowship—until the situation in Brazil was normal again. He never considered himself a political refugee; he had no interest in political causes. Nor was he the typical would-be immigrant who wanted to live in the United States; he had work to do, colonial treasures to save, and three grown daughters at home. But he fell in love, and that changed everything.

Final word about the job in Mexico was expected to come in about two months. In the meantime, after his cultural mission ended, he headed for Lisbon to work on his research there. He wrote to me almost every day on his portable Olivetti, telling me about his experiences in sensitive detail and revealing his deep tenderness. But first he would fill the pages with pen-and-ink sketches of the places he had seen. Then he would wrap his typewritten text around the drawings. Below are excerpts from one of my favorites, which I have translated into English. The first time I read it, I didn't get the point to his little joke—I had been jilted too many times.

Lisbon, Monday, September 7th

Muriel,

I had a wonderful week-end. I went to the south of Portugal and crossed the border to visit a small town in Spain. Along the way, I suddenly realized there was someone with me. She was a young American woman, tall, very gentle, with curious turned-up eyes like the Chinese. They looked pretty when she smiled. Right away we began to talk, and soon we were friends.

...

Arriving in the border town of Vila Real de Santo António, we took a walk and came to a small street closed to traffic with open-air cafés and restaurants on each side. We chose one of the tables and sat down. I drew the sketch below. It didn't turn out very well because she kept watching me. I felt uncomfortable and self-conscious. It's a row of houses from the eighteenth century. I kept the paper to write a letter on it afterwards to someone I love very much.

Spain called to us from the other side of the river, and we got on a ferry that took us across. All the time we were holding hands and pressing tight against each other because the boat was small and crowded.

The woman liked to walk--I forgot to mention that. We walked and walked and then stopped for an early supper. At dusk we took the ferry back to Portugal. I was very happy, and I know that she was, too. We sat down in a plaza at the river's edge, surrounded by flowers, and we kissed. And then we went to bed.

On the way back to Lisbon I realized that the young woman had gone. I was sad after that and felt tired and empty.

--Oh, I forgot to tell you: her name was MURIEL. She said that she lives at 1802 Corcoran Street in Washington, D.C.

As I read it, I felt pangs of jealousy and wondered why he was telling me about his tryst with another woman. When I got to the end and saw my name, I laughed out loud with surprise and relief. Though the surprise was over, I re-read it many times.

When he came back from Portugal, we got to know each other better. I learned that I could count on him. I hadn't known what it was like to place my trust in someone until I met Sylvio. Until then, I literally *expected* that people, especially men, were going to let me down. It had started with my father—the absent sea captain who, when he was in port, often forgot to let Mother and me know that he wouldn't be able to see us. As a small child, I couldn't fault my father, so my job was to not show that I hurt. My mother left him just before I turned four and created a new family with her sister Muriel (whose name I bear) in California.

Mother and Aunt Muriel spent much of their time trying to prove that they were always kind and forgiving, and I thought that was how I was supposed to act. Over the years, people would stand me up, cut me off, break their word, take advantage of me, say cruel things, and I would let them come back and back again. I believed it was the only way to keep them in my life. That they didn't belong in my life never occurred to me. I never understood that I was letting people know I was a person who could be treated that way.

Sylvio saw someone different: a woman who deserved his love and commitment. He constantly presented evidence that I could rely on him. He gently trained me to understand that he was on my side. He would listen. He not only gave me complete emotional security, he was always where he said he would be, and on time.

I remember one day I hailed a cab and told the driver:

"Take me to Nineteenth and L Street—to the tall man in a blue sweater standing on the northeast corner."

If felt so wonderful to be able to say that. We arrived at the intersection, and Sylvio was there, as he said he would be, in his blue sweater.

When we learned that his recruitment papers were on track at the OAS, we decided to get married. We flew down to Laredo, Texas, and crossed the border to Nuevo Laredo, where we were married by a justice of the peace. It was a hasty affair, and we returned to Washington that night.

The next evening, I had an invitation to a formal reception at the grand Hall of the Americas in the old Pan American Union building. We showed up as a married couple and surprised a lot of people.

The job in Mexico City came through a few weeks later, and with it, the coveted G-4 visa, good for the duration of Sylvio's employment with the organization. He was safe!

I gave notice at the office and lined up free-lance work that I could do in Mexico. We found tenants for the little house on Corcoran Street, shipped some basic furniture ahead, and put the rest of my things in storage.

Sylvio bought a Mercury Cougar convertible. It was fire-engine red with white upholstery and quite unlike anything either of us had ever owned. We packed up the trunk and headed for our new home.

Though we each brought to the marriage a recent history of challenge and struggle, the opportunity for a fresh start together gave us optimism. Sylvio often said that nothing was more important in life than the relationship with one's partner: children grow up, leave home, and become good friends if we are lucky. Our marriage meant everything to him—and to me, as well.

We had each yearned for a partner who could match our own singularity and emotional intensity, and we had actually found one. There was unconditional acceptance. We were not afraid of being unloved if we revealed our flaws and mistakes. Being totally accepted by the other made us feel less critical of ourselves. We were not alone in our differentness. This bond protected us from the memories of childhood bullies and from the grown-ups who otherwise might have hurt us.

5

W E ARRIVED IN MEXICO CITY in our red Cougar convertible on January 16, 1971. I have good memories of our life there. In many ways, it had a dream-like quality. It was like an extended honeymoon—until the day when fate would deal us a low blow.

We found a third-floor apartment with a wall of windows facing Paseo de la Reforma, the city's grandest boulevard. It was directly across from the heart of the elegant Zona Rosa ("Pink Zone"), where Sylvio's office was located. We were inside a romantic cocoon. At the time, the Zona Rosa was an upscale tourist mecca, and we often explored its vibrant streets lined with four-star restaurants and luxury shops. The walk west from our apartment led past the U.S. Embassy and on to beautiful Chapultepec Park.

Our apartment was spacious and very empty. The kitchen had pinky-orange metal cabinets but little else. Appliances had been purchased back in Washington and were on their way, along with the few pieces of furniture we had decided to bring. We expected the shipment to arrive in a few days, but it got held up in Mexican Customs, and we found ourselves camping out in the empty apartment for three months with nothing but a makeshift bed, two stools, and a broom, to which Sylvio lashed a light bulb.

Sylvio always came home for lunch. He would leave his office exactly at noon, and I would watch for him from the window as he crossed the avenue's many lanes and medians. In fact, throughout the years we almost always had lunch together. He would not accept an invitation unless I was invited, too—which once put me at the speakers' table at a Rotary Club luncheon, the only woman in a large room full of Mexican men.

Our shipment finally arrived at the end of April. Raindrops were falling, the first of the rainy season. The soft fresh scent felt both soothing and full of promise after the long dry winter—a welcome reward for a patient wait, like a metaphor for the furniture and boxes. I was excited. At last I had raw material to make a home of. At least we had the basics.

With our things around us, we could start having a normal life. I hired a live-in maid who cleaned, did the laundry, shopped, and fixed the meals for the equivalent of $55 a month, a good wage by Mexican standards. Everyone I knew had at least one maid. I didn't have to cook unless I wanted to, but I had been given a cookbook by an American woman married to a Brazilian,[10] like me, and I enjoyed trying out Sylvio's favorite dishes: pork loin and prunes, salt cod with potatoes and onions, heart-of-palm pie, chicken and okra stew, shrimp with chayote, cornmeal mush, and collards in bacon fat, to mention a few. I wanted my efforts to *matar saudades*—assuage his homesickness and fill any void he might be feeling. Having a maid meant that homemaking was an option, not a duty, and I found it very freeing.

Sylvio's height got the Mexicans' attention. Vendors addressed him in English and appeared to think he was a rich American tourist. Once I tried to buy a shirt for him at an upscale department store, Liverpool, but when I gave his measurements to the clerk, she informed me:

"*No vendemos a gigantes*"—We don't cater to giants.

As she walked away, she turned her head and added:

"*Ni a gringos tampoco.*"

So she didn't like Americans, either. I felt stung by her strong prejudice, directed at both Sylvio and me. It reminded me of our conversation in the beginning and his perception that people resented his height. The experience made us feel closer. It was us against the world.

We did have a problem—or at least I did. He was a heavy smoker. I don't recall if I ever told him how much it bothered me. In those days, nonsmokers didn't complain. We were not yet empowered to speak up, so we suffered in silence. I think he understood that it was hard on me, but he didn't, or couldn't, stop. He had had tuberculosis as a young man, contracted during his bohemian days, and had spent a long time in a sanatorium. The doctors collapsed both his lungs and told him that his prognosis was poor: he would never live to see old age. So he always believed he was on borrowed time. Given that history, it seemed inconceivable to me that he would keep on smoking, but he did.

At the end of 1971 we flew back to Virginia to spend the holidays with my mother and aunt. They lived in the countryside on 49 acres of hilly woodland bisected by a stream, not far from Winchester. In addition to celebrating Christmas with my family, Sylvio wanted us to have a proper wedding in the United States, in a church. My family was not religious, but my mother found a Methodist pastor who had a little church that looked like the classic American icon, with white clapboard siding, a sloping roof on each side, and a steeple in front. We set the date.

Sylvio and my mother didn't have a language in common, but they communicated perfectly. The day before the service, he wanted to go shopping and asked her to come along to "interpret." What he really wanted was moral support. They were gone for quite a while, and when they came back, Mother took me aside and said:

"Sylvio has gotten you something very expensive. I will be really upset with you if you complain about the money he spent!"

Late the next afternoon we had our little service in the dimly lit church with only a few candles casting shadows on the walls, my mother and aunt as our witnesses. After the vows and wedding rings were exchanged and it was time to kiss the bride, Sylvio slipped a solitaire diamond ring on my finger. It was beautiful and flashed radiant sparks in the fading light. Because it meant so much to him, it meant that much more to me. We were now really truly married.

Though Sylvio had a valid visa, worries about the future—where our place was to be on the planet—were always in the back of our minds. As his wife, I applied for his "green card," which would grant him the permanent right to live and work in the United States. But the process dragged on for several reasons. For example, we found out that his file had gotten comingled with that of another Sylvio de Vasconcellos who was also applying for a U.S. visa. As a result, the security investigation had run into some facts that didn't match up. Straightening out the confusion added to the delay. That was just one of many roadblocks we had to deal with.

While daily afternoon rains in the summer made Mexico City fresh, green, and livable, the winters were dry and windy, and air pollution was one of our biggest challenges. It was very hard on Sylvio's lungs. The air was thick with dust—a blend of vehicle exhaust, factory emissions, and pulverized household waste from millions of squatters on a dried-up salt flat east of the city, one of the largest slums in the world. [11] Visibility was so poor in winter that sometimes we couldn't see to drive the car.

Another source of pollution was airborne toxins from numerous construction sites. A new building was being erected next to ours, and one day the air filled up with particles of asbestos, like a heavy snowstorm. They stung when they touched the skin and left red spots that burned for a couple of days. We looked as if we had measles, and we were both having trouble breathing, so we took an unplanned vacation and got out of town. It's quite possible that we both suffered permanent lung damage from that asbestos shower.

In the meantime, Sylvio was developing a growth on his neck and the top of his chest that made it difficult to wear ties. I noticed it was getting bigger, but he would get annoyed when I mentioned it, so I let the matter drop. Because he didn't want to talk about it, there was little I could do. Seeing him all the time and feeding him three hearty meals a day, I hadn't noticed that he was losing a lot of weight. It was only when I saw a photo of him in the newspaper that I realized how gaunt he had become. Shortly after the photo appeared, he came home from work one evening and announced:

"I've got to get out of here. The air is killing me."

That was the beginning of our complicated departure from Mexico. We decided to leave right away, instead of waiting for the end of his two-year contract, and hope for the best.

After some nudging, his green card application came up for review and he was asked to report to the U.S. Consulate. They did a medical examination and ran a series of tests. A week later they called him in again and informed him that he had active tuberculosis.

They could not give him a green card.

Sylvio kept his feelings to himself, but I was devastated. We asked for a copy of the lab results, and I made an appointment for him to see a lung specialist. I, for one, wanted confirmation. And if he really had active tuberculosis, I wanted more information about his disease and guidance on what we had to do next.

When we got to the doctor's office, Sylvio refused to go inside. He stayed downstairs on the sidewalk. I went ahead and kept the appointment so that I could get answers to my questions. The doctor looked at the papers and said flatly:

"*No hay ni vuelta de hoja.*" That was a Mexican expression which meant that there's no point in turning the page; it's an open-and-shut case. The culture tests showed a mass of *M. tuberculosis* germs. The doctor explained that their large number meant that his lungs were actively infected. He gave me a prescription for the drugs that Sylvio would have to take, one of which had to be injected.

Sylvio was waiting outside with a bouquet of flowers in his hand.

Simply put, the bottom had dropped out of our life. If the air in Mexico was killing him, his visa in the United States was tied to a job that was about to end, and prison was waiting for him in Brazil, there was no place to go.

What we did next was not exactly legal. In Mexico, you don't have to surrender your prescription to the pharmacist, so I held onto the one the doctor had given me and went from pharmacy to pharmacy until I had stockpiled the full course of treatment. Our plan was for Sylvio to fly up to my family's home in Virginia and undergo his treatment there. The air would be clean and fresh, which he desperately needed, and most important, he would bypass any future hurdles that might keep him from entering the United States.

To get permission for Sylvio to leave his job in Mexico, a friend who was a urologist wrote a certificate for a medical leave of absence based on a diagnosis of "stress."

I also called up the rear guard: my mother came to help. Her presence made us feel that we weren't lost and alone in our challenge. She also provided much-needed relief for me, as I was translating at a conference and trying to finish up some other assignments. She made sure that Sylvio got his meals, played cards with him in the evenings, and helped me box up our belongings.

At the end of her visit, the two of them got on a plane together, with the stockpile of medicines in Sylvio's luggage.

He had not been in Virginia long when he began to feel better. A neighbor who was a nurse came by regularly to give him his injections and supervise his treatment.

Meanwhile, I turned my attention to closing up the apartment. I finished packing and watched the movers load up our furniture and boxes. Then I stuffed everything that was left into the car and headed north to catch up with Sylvio. I made the 2,440-mile trip in less than three days.

6

NEITHER MY FAMILY NOR THE nurse seemed to be concerned that Sylvio might be contagious. As for me, that was the least of my worries. Between the treatment and the fresh country air, he quickly began to feel better. But I was in Washington, having already found a new job, and his office was waiting for him to report to work. As we had hoped, his supervisors at the OAS (unaware of his diagnosis) had arranged for him to finish out his contract at headquarters. So he cut his treatment short and came into town to resume his duties.

I had been able to get a job with my previous employer, but I was just a copy editor—not exactly the work I had wanted. With the house on Corcoran Street occupied, we rented a small furnished studio across from my office. The good news was that we both had jobs with health insurance, and Sylvio's G-4 visa was still valid, for a while at least.

With health insurance secured, we were able to address the growth on Sylvio's neck, which had become the size and shape of a child's football and was extremely noticeable. He underwent surgery, and a large fatty tumor extending from his neck to the top of his left lung was removed. I never understood what caused it, but we were told it was neither tuberculous nor cancerous—and luckily, the tests did not show any TB germs.

While Sylvio was still on sick leave recovering from his surgery, his grown daughters Andréa and Cláudia came up from Brazil for a two-week visit. We managed to cram everyone into the studio apartment. Sometimes I worried that he was still too weak for the adventures we embarked on, but their visit was the tonic he needed. For me, it was my first opportunity to build a bond with his daughters, which has grown over the years.

After the girls left, Sylvio went back to work once again. We were praying his contract would be extended; otherwise, his visa would expire and he could not remain in the country. We were back to the same old anxieties. There was always the fear that he might be forced to return to Brazil, where he still faced the threat of prison.

Despite our worries, we managed to settle into a routine. We had friends and were regulars at the Brazilian-American Cultural Institute. We loved to hang out in Georgetown, where we would window-shop, explore side streets, or sit in cafés and just talk. Talking was always our favorite pastime. And we always held hands.

On a business trip to Colombia, Sylvio bought me an emerald ring, since emerald is my birthstone. The fit was loose, and I was carrying it in my wallet with the intention of having it resized. One day my wallet was stolen, the ring with it. I cried because it had meant so much to me. The next day he came home with *another* emerald ring. The stone was more than three times the size of the one I had lost. When I saw it, I was so touched and overwhelmed that I cried all over again. He feigned frustration:

"But I got it for you so you'd stop crying!"

Sylvio's contract ended at the OAS. A new one was in the works, but in the meantime we bit our fingernails and reactivated the application for his green card. Now there were *two* things to worry about: not only getting the wheels of bureaucracy to start turning again, but also demonstrating that he had a clean bill of health. Since his tuberculosis wasn't active when he had surgery, we assumed he was in the clear.

He adjusted easily to his new schedule. He was rich in inner resources, and he loved to write. His favorite thing to do was churn out text on his sturdy little portable. In the course of his career, he wrote fourteen books and hundreds of shorter pieces—articles, essays, and columns—that appeared in journals, magazines, and newspapers in Brazil and elsewhere. I translated some of the articles into English. [12]

His new hobby was sketching. He claimed that his letters to me from Portugal had gotten him started. He used a crow-quill pen and india ink, and his fine lines captured the most minute details. His control of the pen always amazed me. Over the years, we put together at least half a dozen one-man exhibits.

For my part, I had started teaching translation at Georgetown University. Standing in front of a classroom was a new experience for me, but Sylvio, who had taught architecture, gave me wise pointers. Most important, he believed, was to treat students with respect. Any question deserved a thoughtful answer. The rest was secondary. I would come home from class exhilarated, feeling I had done a good job. I grew to love this work, though correcting homework took up a lot of my time and the pay barely covered my expenses. I ended up teaching classes at Georgetown for 14 years.

I was also doing volunteer work for a translators' association, first as treasurer and then as executive secretary. Sylvio didn't get the point. He believed that no generous deed goes unpunished, especially in volunteer organizations, and he urged me to stop. I promised him I would wind up my pending tasks and step down. The day I resigned, I came home to find a pair of diamond earrings screwed to a cutout of me that he had created on cardstock.

We often spent week-ends with my mother and aunt in Virginia. My relationship with Aunt Muriel had always been somewhat strained. I definitely felt the burden of being named for her. At home, I was "Little Muriel" and she was "Big Muriel," and everyone thought it was funny because I was tall and she was short. She had a Ph.D. in psychology and was well known in her specialized field, and she often brought important people home for dinner. She knew Eleanor Roosevelt and fostered contact with eminent professionals around the world. She constantly name-dropped and place-dropped. Though she projected a sweet and caring do-gooder persona, the reality was that she treated Mother like a servant and she was often quite short with me.

Sylvio handled the situation with great diplomacy. He knew how to make her feel important while at the same time letting

Mother and me feel that his true loyalties lay with us. We would play cards in the evening, and Sylvio would partner with Aunt Muriel. He was an excellent player and Aunt Muriel was hopeless, while Mother was very good and I was mediocre, so the two sides balanced out. Sylvio made Aunt Muriel laugh and act silly, and it softened my heart when I saw her having so much fun. She was very proud of her charming and handsome nephew-in-law.

Aunt Muriel was a close friend of Margaret Mead, the anthropologist, who had been a fixture in my life since childhood. My aunt worshipped her. They co-wrote a book, *The Wagon and the Star*.[13] Sometimes Sylvio and I would pick up Dr. Mead and drive her out to the country. She and Sylvio clicked. She thought he was wonderful. She would hang onto every word of his stumbling English (or my translations) and laugh at his pithy remarks. I remember one of his pearls that she thought was especially wise:

"Americans have nostalgia for the past they never had."

I was glad that Sylvio had the opportunity to know Dr. Mead. She was a fascinating person. She loved to talk about the burning topics of the day—women's rights, abortion, politics, religion . . . nothing was off limits—and she always brought a new perspective. She was interested in what everyone had to say, and everyone was important to her. Once we took her to Dulles Airport to catch a plane and she was quickly surrounded by a crowd. As she sat waiting for her flight, people huddled around her on the floor and listened raptly as she answered their questions about the world and how to fix it. If we went out to dinner, people would recognize her with her famous forked walking stick and ask for her autograph. She would beam; she enjoyed her fame.

Sylvio's new contract had come through with the OAS, and with it, renewal of his G-4 visa. Though his visa was valid again, our sights were still set on getting a green card. For over three years the papers for his renewed application had been inching their way through the red tape.

By late spring 1975 his file was in order and he was granted an appointment at the U.S. Consulate in Mexico City. The interview was a formality; presumably he would pass the TB test and be granted the visa. We packed our bags and flew down. It was summer, and Mexico City looked green and tropical. We had a nice time and enjoyed catching up with our friends.

The Consulate had not forgotten that Sylvio had health issues. Before the appointment, they did a complete physical exam and tested him again for tuberculosis. On the day of the actual appointment, without explanation they handed him a large sealed envelope containing a set of X-rays and other papers and told him to turn it in to the Immigration Service in Miami. They also took his picture and gave him a temporary card. It wasn't clear if we were "home free," but we didn't want to stir up trouble by asking questions.

When we landed in Miami, the first immigration officer took the envelope, glanced at its contents, and greeted us warmly:

"One returning citizen. One new resident. Welcome to the United States!"

He smiled at Sylvio, and Sylvio smiled back. I felt both relieved and honored. I fought back tears.

At the next window, the second officer opened the envelope again and looked more closely at the papers. He then directed us to a room behind a door that bore the seal of the U.S. Public Health Service. We sat down and waited, nervously. Time passed, and we missed our connecting flight to Washington. After what seemed an eternity, I went and asked a woman what we were waiting for. She checked with her supervisor, and no one seemed to know why we were there, so she told us we could leave. We picked up our things and started to walk toward the check-in counters to find a new flight. At first we walked normally, then we picked up our pace. Within minutes, the loudspeaker started to blare:

"Sylvio Vasconcellos. Sylvio Vasconcellos. Please report to the U.S. Public Health Service. Sylvio Vasconcellos . . ."

Neither of us hesitated: we took one quick look at each other, and without a word we broke into a run. As if by a miracle, we immediately found a flight headed for Washington with a pair of empty seats. Sylvio's name was still being called as we boarded.

Safe at home after our "escape," we waited anxiously to learn what was going to happen next. Would he be quarantined? Deported? Silence. For two long months we heard nothing. Then one day, quietly and unannounced, his permanent card arrived in the regular mail. It was nicely laminated, and the background color was blue after all, not green. We celebrated.

By this time we had been together for five years and we had faced one uncertainty after another. In our struggle to deal with the challenges, our intense focus left almost no room for disagreements. When we had them, they were quickly forgotten. We knew our priorities: we had big things to worry about, and the little ones didn't matter. We were two romantics. We both idealized the relationship, and we were prepared to overlook many things that otherwise might have bothered us.

7

IN THE FALL OF 1975, we moved back into the house on Corcoran Street. We felt more grounded there, in the heart of Dupont Circle. It's a delightful walkable neighborhood, with narrow tree-lined streets, early nineteenth century row houses, and many shops and cafés.

For our Christmas card that year, Sylvio sketched the façade of the house and cut out a flap for the front door, revealing a snapshot of the two of us.

I rode my bicycle to work. It was the perfect solution to the parking problem. One day my bike was gone. Though it was locked, someone had managed to lift it over the post it was attached to. Sylvio surprised me by buying me a new one. He found an identical match. Once again, he tried to make things right for me.

Of course, we didn't always see eye to eye. Sylvio chose to have few possessions, and he was troubled by my accumulation of treasures. That was one of our few bones of contention. The house had a large attic, and I kept the things we weren't using out of sight. From time to time, he would climb to the top of the pull-down ladder and look around to see what I had collected. What he saw invariably put him in a bad mood. I suggested that he would be better off not looking, but of course that wasn't the point. He claimed it was a safety issue, that the ceiling might cave in. But the real truth was that he had a horror of stuff that didn't have a purpose and a place.

We had been back on Corcoran Street for just a few months when I discovered my lump and began to worry about having cancer. That was also the time when my employment situation took a turn for the worse and I lost out on the promotion in my own organization. So from my perspective, our new life wasn't turning out to be as easy as I had hoped it would be.

Sylvio, for his part, was planning to wind up his last contract with the OAS early the following year. This time he meant it. He was tired of working 40 hours a week. Though he was only 59, he was looking forward to being retired. He had his small pension from the Brazilian government and some money saved up, and he reasoned that he needed quality time more than money. Though he could be a hard worker, whenever he had work to do, he would rush to finish it so that he could *ficar a toa*—take it easy. At least that's what he called it. What he cared about was having the freedom to pursue his creative talents, because he was rarely idle. When he did relax, he relaxed completely. He was always hoping that I would do the same.

Over the years he had insisted he really didn't want a job, and at first I had difficulty understanding that. Raised with a strong work ethic, I actually thought he was rationalizing. Also, our age difference meant that we were going through different phases of life. But the understanding slowly came to me. By the time we moved back to Corcoran Street, I was ready to honor his goals and accept that not having a job was what he truly wanted—and that it was all right for him to stay home.

He had plenty to do. He continued to write feverishly. In his column, which appeared three times a week in Brazil,[14] he wrote musings about life in general and life in the United States in particular, and he told stories with tongue in cheek. Sometimes they were hilarious. His main motivation for writing the columns was to create a presence back home so that his daughters would feel that their dad was "somebody," even if he couldn't be there. It was his way of supporting them from afar.

He was also writing book chapters and articles in his areas of expertise for various journals and magazines. He could write more than twice as fast as I could unravel his tightly crafted language to translate it.

A week or so before Christmas, I happened to notice a carbon copy of his holiday column lying on a table. Naturally, I read it. In it, he said that he was grateful for all that he had, which was more than anything he had ever aspired to. But there was still one thing he wanted—a dog. One that was his alone. It should be large enough to be a "real" dog but still *portátil*, so that he could pick it up and carry it in an emergency. He liked long ears. Yes, a Cocker Spaniel would be perfect.

I wasted no time reaching for the classifieds in the day's paper. Only one Cocker Spaniel was listed for sale: a six-month-old black female—more specifically, an English Cocker. All I needed was one. Inventing an excuse for my whereabouts, I went to have a look at her. She was quite pretty, with a white star on her forehead, and she was sweet and friendly. She had been named

Sunshine, possibly to cheer her up, as she did have rather sad eyes. I decided to get her.

It was my turn to surprise Sylvio. She was my gift to him, to brighten his upcoming retirement. With my family's help, we kept her hidden until Christmas morning. After all the other presents had been opened, my mother brought her in, popping out of a makeshift "chimney" and sporting a Santa hat and a red velvet bow. Sylvio was overcome with emotion; he hid his face to conceal his tears. From that day on, she was his dog. He would take her for long walks, and then they would settle down next to each other on a bench or step and people-watch or contemplate their universe. She was his alone, and she never left his side, just as he had always wanted.

8

SUNSHINE HAD ONLY BEEN WITH us briefly when I had my partial mastectomy in January 1977. At first, losing out on the job I wanted, even more than the diagnosis, was casting a pall on our lives. By mid-March, my six weeks of radiation were over, but spring had not yet arrived. Everything was bleak: the sky, the trees, my attitude.

I had a bad case of bronchitis, but at least the surgery and radiation were behind me. Other than an ugly scar and an unbalanced bosom, there was nothing to remind me that I had had cancer.

By that time Sylvio had stopped working. I wanted to be home with him and dreaded going in to work.

The organization's medical referee had learned about my diagnosis and called me into his office. This man was a shadowy figure who made arbitrary decisions about our fitness for employment, and I never really understood who he was working for. From the start of the conversation, I felt uncomfortable. He had a reputation for being nosy, so I wasn't surprised when he told me that he knew about the other job I had applied for and my rejection for insurance reasons.

He asked me why I wasn't happy in my current job. I stumbled through a vague answer, being careful not to say anything that might get passed on to Personnel and go in my file. Then the interrogation got even more intrusive. He started asking about my sex life and wanted to know why Sylvio and I hadn't had children. By that time I was squirming in my seat and looking for the nearest exit. Though he wasn't responsible for the decision not to hire me for the other job (at least I don't think he was), I felt I was at his mercy—and by extension, at the mercy of a much larger "system." In concluding the interview, he summed up my situation in terms that raised my discouragement to the level of despair:

"You may as well face it. With your diagnosis, no insurance company will cover you and no one will hire you. You will never be able to work anywhere else. You are locked in."

His words rang in my ears for weeks. I was in a new prison. I had spent nine months trapped in an ordeal of uncertainty; now it was the opposite, the certainty of knowing that I was stuck in the same place for the rest of my working life. The effect was the same: frustration and anger, which built up in a feedback loop that kept making me feel more desperate. I cried. Sylvio tried to comfort me.

I considered becoming an activist. I wanted to change the world so that no one would ever be denied health insurance.

In the meantime, my job situation was getting increasingly difficult. While my supervisor, Clara, was solicitous about my health and stopped by my desk every morning to ask how I was doing, on another level our differences over the content of the journal were escalating. Anything she wasn't used to was hard for her to accept. If I tried something creative, she always squashed it. One time she got really angry when I suggested grouping three articles on a particular subject in the same issue. She thought it was a terrible idea; we would lose readers. So of course we did it her way. Another time, she asked me to write a 1,500-word article on population growth. After she read it, she called me in and slowly and deliberately slashed a diagonal line across each page:

"We can't use this. The problem is, it's too well written."

I hadn't understood: she wanted something bland and really vague. We had been mandated to publish a piece about population growth, but, according to Clara, we were not to imply that it posed any challenges. I couldn't tell whether her concern was political or religious, or whether my style was simply too emphatic. I was careful to stay away from the subject after that.

Clara also insisted that I publish articles that I had decided to reject. One, I remember, was more than ten years old, and another was thin on substance. I became righteous. Matters came to a head when she demanded that I sign off on some changes she made that I didn't agree with. I resisted; she prevailed. I went home in tears.

Sylvio was my port in a storm. He was always on my side when I came home from the office upset. It felt wonderful to come home to him. We were so close that we often had the same thoughts and finished each other's sentences. One warm afternoon in late spring, the weather was so nice that I decided to go home early. I was going to surprise him. When I arrived, he wasn't there. He showed up about an hour later. It turned out that he had had the same idea and had gone to my office to talk me into taking the rest of the day off! The joy of being with him made the situation at the office seem all the more unpleasant by comparison.

The episode with Clara that brought me to tears was the last straw. It got me thinking outside the box, and I hatched a plan to create a different job for myself within the organization. I had heard that the director for administration was keenly interested in computer applications to streamline the translation task and was actually exploring the use of machine translation. I had some background in that area from my days at Georgetown. I also saw the need for a database of standardized terms in the organization's working languages. I went to him directly, bypassing the levels in between, and offered to coordinate both efforts. I proposed a half-time job. If I could keep all my benefits and continue contributing to the retirement fund, I said I would be willing to work fewer hours for proportionately less pay. He liked the idea and started the ball rolling.

The real challenge was getting management to agree to part-time employment. Even though the rules allowed for it and actually spelled out the procedures, there was no precedent. It threw everyone a curve. People thought I was crazy. They tried to talk me out of it. No one in their right mind would volunteer to take home less money. I had to argue my case at every level.

Through it all, my real goal was to spend more time with Sylvio. Since my surgery, we were closer than we had ever been.

Eventually a half-time position was created with the duties I had in mind. I worked every morning from 8:30 to 12:30, and I took my work seriously.

At home with Sylvio, I was ready to devote full measure to our life together. In a spirit of making every minute count, we filled our time with a mix of pleasure and purpose. On the pleasure side, we took drives, watched sailboats at the marina, went to movies, sat in cafés and made up stories about the people at the other tables, took in museums and art shows, and spent time with our friends.

At the same time, we both became more purposeful. Sylvio started to write a book. His subject was the eighteenth century Brazilian sculptor and architect, Antônio Francisco Lisboa. He deplored his subject's nickname "Aleijadinho," or "Little Cripple," and was intent on dispelling myths and setting the record straight.

For my part, after a 19-year absence from graduate school, I returned to work on my master's degree at Georgetown in the summer of 1977. Though Sylvio missed my presence at home, he had been encouraging me to do this for some time. He couldn't relate to bureaucracies, but he understood academia. He saw a master's degree as a contribution toward job security and leverage for more opportunities in my current workplace. Also, we had both thought it would be nice if I could get a teaching job with summers off. That was before. Now I knew I probably couldn't be hired because of my diagnosis, but pursuing my interest and taking part in academic life was a stimulating change and just the prescription I needed. While Sylvio hadn't expected me to get so deeply involved, he still approved.

In addition to these commitments, Sylvio and I also embarked on a project that we worked on together. We applied for, and won, a grant from the National Endowment for the Humanities to translate a set of three historical Brazilian documents from the eighteenth century. I translated the texts and Sylvio annotated them with extensive footnotes.

And so it turned out that, despite my reduced schedule at the office, I was still burning the candle at both ends: squeezing in my studies, correcting papers or doing freelance translations in the early morning or late at night, and saving the afternoon to work with Sylvio on our joint project. Cancer took a back seat; I was too busy doing and thinking about other things.

Sylvio worried that I wasn't getting enough sleep. He offered to pay me 10 cents for every minute I went to bed before 11 o'clock. I realized that I was short-changing myself, and I thought that money might be an incentive for me to better my ways. So I agreed to his proposal and started keeping a careful record of my bedtimes. There was a definite improvement in my schedule, and I began to have more energy. I was also accumulating some credit. After a couple of months, I presented him with my bill. He looked at it quizzically and said:

"Oh, I didn't mean I was actually going to *pay* you. The point was for you to get more sleep. That's your reward."

I couldn't be mad at him. I had to laugh, and I was touched by his logic. But I stopped keeping track, and I lost my incentive to go to bed early.

Sylvio captured the essence of my schedule on our 1977 Christmas card.

One day Sunshine managed to get into my 1911 collector's edition of the Encyclopedia Britannica. This reference provided excellent historical details for our project, and I had about ten volumes spread out on the bed (space was at a premium in our little house). We went out for dinner and came home to find the tissue-thin pages shredded into tiny bits. Sylvio knew how much I valued the encyclopedia. Always trying to make things right for me, he went and bought a shopping bag full of transparent adhesive tape. Together we spent hours carefully mending the damaged pages. I felt it was a metaphor for all we had gone through. We had both spent so much time trying to put pieces back together again, for each other more than for ourselves.

9

B Y 1978 OUR MAJOR WORRIES were behind us: Sylvio's permanent residency, his tuberculosis, my cancer, my job situation, his retirement—all had been taken care of. We were secure. Even better, we were both happily doing what we liked to do best—sometimes together, sometimes separately.

We became landlords. We bought a one-bedroom condo in suburban Virginia for $17,500, fixed it up, and rented it out. We reasoned that the rent would be a nice addition to our monthly income, and the value of the property was certain to increase.

In early summer, Sylvio's eldest daughter, Andréa, came to spend a month with us. She was a strikingly beautiful young woman. It was probably the longest time she ever spent alone with her father without competition from her sisters, and I think the opportunity gave her a sense of security and fulfillment that she had longed for—and a generosity of spirit. She reached out and included me in subtle ways that moved me deeply. After she left, I found a note on her pillow in the guest room. Translated, it said: "Dad and Muriel: I love you both, and I need you both."

Later that summer we saw Margaret Mead for the last time. She had been diagnosed with pancreatic cancer and was being treated at the National Institutes of Health. We picked her up at NIH and took her out to the country to see my aunt. She had made the commitment to see all her close friends and say good-bye in person. She and my aunt took a short trip together. She returned to New York to spend her last weeks in her apartment facing Central Park. She refused further treatment, which greatly upset those who cared about her, including my aunt, who had hoped that treatment would pull her through, or at least extend her life. I actually admired Dr. Mead's decision. It gave me the opportunity to think seriously about the question of treatment versus quality of life when time is so short and precious. She died in November, and Sylvio and I attended the service for her at the National Cathedral.

Aunt Muriel was too devastated to go to the service. Afterwards, she fell into a deep depression. For nearly 40 years Dr. Mead had been the juice that kept her going. She adored her. She was thrilled beyond measure to be a part of her life, and the reflected glory had been warm and exciting. Now her world was barren.

Today Dr. Mead's name shows up on "Jeopardy" and in crossword puzzles, and visitors at the New York Museum of Natural History can see exhibits from her life and work. But her gigantic energy and magnetism can only be appreciated by those who knew her or saw her speak in person. For Aunt Muriel, the loss left a hole from which she never recovered.

Sylvio and I took a trip to Portugal in August and September. Our grant proposal had included money to do research there. I was eager to see the country first-hand; he had been talking about it for as long as I had known him. He wanted to show me the sights he was so familiar with—the places he had sketched and written to me about, and where he had even taken me along in his imagination.

When we arrived in Lisbon, I had never seen him so enthusiastic. We did our research there, and we also combed the fabric of the city—every street, every ancient byway, all of Sylvio's old haunts. I recognized many of the places from the sketches in his letters. I remember Lisbon for its tiled façades and murals, the fine porcelain, the exuberant pottery; the collard soup, broiled squid, and "green" wine; the sad ballads, or *fados*; the ubiquitous women in mourning; swans swimming in the median of Avenida da Liberdade and white peacocks on the grounds of Saint George's Castle; and the clusters of men loitering on the sidewalk, with Sylvio stopping to ask for a light so that he could strike up a conversation. It was his culture, and he fit in perfectly.

From Lisbon we rented a car and set out to roam the countryside. We made a special pilgrimage to the magnificent Alcobaça Monastery, where Sylvio traced his roots, both genealogically and sentimentally.[15] He wanted to pay tribute to the cruelly murdered Inês de Castro, whose body was later exhumed so she could be crowned Queen of Portugal. Sylvio, always moved by the restitution of justice, saw the coronation of Inês as the ultimate righting of a wrong.

Coimbra was the home of Sylvio's nursemaid, Olympia. I especially remember walking along the banks of the Mondego River at nightfall and he sang the songs she had taught him in his deep resonant bass.

Our journey ended in the city of Porto. We had many adventures along the way. While Sylvio knew Portugal like the back of his hand, seeing it with me had been his dream, and the dream came true, more rich and exciting than either of us had imagined.

Back in Washington, the page proofs from Sylvio's book about Antônio Francisco Lisboa were waiting for him. It was scheduled to come out in early 1979.

In the fall, Sylvio started to have episodes of chills and spiking fever. They would develop in a matter of minutes. Once, we were already dressed to go to a dinner party when one of these attacks came on and we had to cancel. He would stay in bed for a few days, and then he would be all right again for a while.

He believed these attacks were related to his past tuberculosis. I made an appointment for him to see a general practitioner. When we explained Sylvio's symptoms, the doctor declared decisively:

"You don't have tuberculosis. It wouldn't come back that way."

As part of the physical exam, he gave Sylvio a cup for a urine specimen and pointed in the direction of the bathroom. Sylvio had not understood; as a well-trained TB patient, he emerged from the bathroom with a sputum sample in the cup. The doctor looked at it and said dismissively:

"Oh, I didn't want *that!*"

He tossed the cup in a wastebasket.

Memories of my own search for a diagnosis came to mind. I made an appointment with a specialist in infectious diseases, who happened to be a woman. Sylvio refused to answer her questions or undress in front of her. He said it was because she was a woman, but I think he was scared, like the time in Mexico when he walked out on the appointment with the lung doctor. Given his resistance, I gave up trying to pursue the matter and hoped that his chills and fever would pass.

Despite this cloud on the horizon, in between the episodes we continued to enjoy every minute of the new life we had created.

It was now almost two years since my surgery, and we had become closer than ever before. Though Dr. Laird had downplayed the seriousness of my cancer, the insurance rejection told me that not everyone was as optimistic as he was. I was beginning to believe that there were reasons to be concerned about my future. We valued our time together as if it were about to end.

10

A S THE BALL DROPPED IN Times Square, Sylvio hugged me hard and declared that 1978 had been the happiest year of his life.

"Our love gets bigger each year," he added in English.

I agreed.

But when the confetti settled and the last notes of Auld Lang Syne had been sung, his mood got more somber: he pointed out that 1979 was an odd-numbered year. According a long-held theory of his, it meant that something bad was going to happen. Good things happen in even years. For example, we met and got married in 1970. But every catastrophe of his life had occurred in an odd year. The record of calamities went back to his childhood and included his imprisonment in 1965. The evidence was so compelling that I almost believed him.

I did see a couple of problems with his theory, however. I realized even then, and came to understand more fully later, that prophesies of this kind can be self-fulfilling. When we focus on something, whether positive or negative, the energy has a way of taking on a life of its own. Molehills become mountains and beget more of the same. Another problem is that ideas like this have a pernicious way of sticking in the back of the mind. I have to confess that I have not been able to shake the memory of Sylvio's calendar-based belief to this day: I still look forward to even years and gird my loins to face the odd ones.

I could also see some merit to the approach. It struck me as a clever strategy for survival: he could tell himself that only the calendar was to be blamed for situations beyond his control. Moreover, there was relief in sight: no matter how grim the picture got, next year everything would be fine. The flip side, of course, was that prosperity didn't last either; he would have to "pay" for his good fortune. But he may have seen a certain sense of rightness to that as well.

As for 1979, Sylvio seriously believed that his luck had run out. He had a premonition that something really awful was going to happen.

January brought the usual post-holiday emptiness. Most of the month was spent fixing up our rental unit. The tenants had broken their lease without notice, leaving the place in shambles. The wall-to-wall carpet was disgusting and had to be replaced. To save the cost of taking it up, Sylvio decided to do the work himself. The exertion was too much for him. Even before he finished, he had started to get one of his attacks of fever. He went to bed for a few days and the episode passed. By early February he was feeling better and the apartment was re-rented. The rest of our activities were minimal. The weather was frigid and we were staying close to home.

Saturday, February 17, was the coldest day of the year so far, and our street was covered with a sheet of ice. It was too narrow for snow plows to come through, and the shade from the surrounding buildings kept the ice from melting. We were marooned. We spent the day talking. Sylvio was excited because he had received a letter from his sister Maria Selma, whom he hadn't heard from in years. She wanted to come and visit us in September, and he was thrilled. She was the sister he had been closest to growing up. He started telling me stories from their childhood. Just before supper, he braved the cold to go out and get cigarettes. I thought he was crazy: the sidewalks and streets were dangerously slick, the wind was blowing, and the temperature was freezing. Most people would have done without.

He didn't feel well the rest of the evening. We turned in around eleven o'clock. After he lay down he started coughing strangely. Something was very different. He got up and went to the bathroom. When he turned on the light, he confirmed what he had suspected: he was coughing up blood.

With an edge of urgency in his voice, he asked me to get him to a hospital. I started to call a taxi, but he interrupted and said: "No. Call 911."

He put a coat on over his pajamas and I quickly threw on a pair of pants and a sweater. In about ten minutes the ambulance pulled up in front of the house, whining in spurts. Neighbors turned on their lights and appeared at windows and doors. We picked our way across the icy sidewalk and climbed into the back, where we sat down side by side on a bench, Sylvio with his head on his knees. As the ambulance doors closed, I saw Sunshine barking frantically in the bay window. We had forgotten to say good-bye and reassure her that we were coming back.

The ride was bumpy and slippery but mercifully short. In five minutes we had arrived at the nearest hospital. Sylvio was quickly admitted as an inpatient. I stayed in his room and slept in a chair that night. A neighbor volunteered to take care of Sunshine.

His condition was monitored, and by the next morning the hospital's top lung specialist was on the case. He explained that sometimes hemorrhaging from the lung—known as *hemoptysis*—can stop on its own if the patient is kept very quiet. In the meantime, they were trying to find the cause. His blood samples contained germs, but they were not *M. tuberculosis*, and no one could identify them. He was the center of attention.

The bleeding did slow down, as the doctors had hoped, but it didn't stop entirely. But by that time he had started to run a fever.

Early Sunday evening it began to snow. Sylvio wanted to watch. He got out of bed and we sat at the window in the dark for the longest time, hands clasped, as it piled up gently but quickly, until soon the parked cars were nothing but white mounds. We felt so close. Again I spent the night, this time because of the weather. In the morning we learned that the city was blanketed with almost 19 inches of snow, the most in a single day since 1899. It remains the city's second heaviest snowfall on record. The snow kept doctors and nurses from reaching the hospital for more than 24 hours, so the personnel who were already there had to keep working without relief. For days the institution reeled from the interruption in its routine.

Through all the excitement around us, I was guardedly optimistic about Sylvio's condition. I took comfort in the explanation that he would probably get better with rest and hospital care—that hemoptysis looked more scary than it really was.

On Monday evening, Sylvio's fever began to spike. He had a severe infection. Samples were sent to the U.S. Centers for Disease Control, and eight weeks later they reported that what he had was a mutant of *M. tuberculosis*,[16] and there was a drug to treat it. I thought: if only the doctor I took him to six months earlier had done his job! He could have tested Sylvio's sputum, instead of throwing it out and declaring that he couldn't possibly have tuberculosis.

Though the doctors knew he had an infection and were treating him with antibiotics, Sylvio was convinced he had cancer. He was deeply depressed. He became angry and grumpy. He was afraid, and at the same time he kept declaring that he wanted to die. Most of all, he was terrified of a prolonged and difficult illness. He repeatedly asked me to promise that no extraordinary measures would be taken to help him hold on to life.

He had no appetite. He hadn't really eaten since he arrived at the hospital. His temperature was still high on Wednesday, and the bleeding from his lungs was worse. He made it no secret that he was miserable, and my heart ached because there was nothing I could do to help him.

Thursday brought continuing fever and more bleeding. He got very quiet, and we spent most of the day in silence. He slept a lot, and I sat close to him so we could hold hands. At one point he gave mine a squeeze and said:

"I can't die, because I can't leave you alone. If it weren't for you, I'm ready to go."

I scoffed at the idea that it was time for him to go and reassured him that worrying about me was not the point—I would always be able to manage.

I went home that night, trudging through deep drifts of snow, to check in on Sunshine and sleep in my own bed. Before dawn the next morning I woke up suddenly. It was four o'clock. I felt very restless and had an urgent sense that I had to get to the hospital. On second thought, I reasoned, I didn't want to wake Sylvio up because he needed the rest. So I actually sat around waiting until six o'clock and arrived at the hospital half an hour later.

If only I had listened to my heart instead of my head! For two hours he had been hemorrhaging massively. They had called in a surgeon, and he was being prepped for surgery.

After four hours, the surgeon finally emerged from the Operating Room. He described what he had found in nonmedical terms:

"I found everything but rats and snakes!"

I could hardly contain my rage. He was crude and disrespectful, and I took a deep dislike to him. I eventually found out that an artery had been severed by a clumped mass of germs. Much later I learned that he probably had severe *cavitation*—cavities that develop in the lungs in the final stage of pulmonary tuberculosis. From other comments the doctor made, it was clear that he blamed Sylvio for his illness, associating it with poor hygiene and an unhealthy lifestyle—and of course, Sylvio was a smoker.

When I got in to see Sylvio in the Intensive Care Unit, he was attached to every machine and apparatus imaginable, including a respirator. The only thing missing was a feeding tube. I was concerned that he had not eaten anything in four days. However, the doctors explained that he would be all right without food and giving it to him now could cause other problems.

By the next morning he was wide awake, and it was clear that he was in pain. As he got better, he wrote me messages and told me where he was hurting. There was always something that hurt.

He could also nod his head, knit his brow, and talk with his eyes. That was how we communicated.

His progress was slow. His left lung had collapsed, and they had trouble getting it to work again. After three days, however, he graduated from the respirator. Once he could talk, I repeated a number of things I had told him before, just to be sure he had heard. At one point, he snapped:

"You've told me that four times already!"

So he hadn't missed a thing.

Though the rule in Intensive Care was that family could visit once an hour for just five minutes, the nurses realized that he was watching the clock and getting impatient in between, so they allowed me to stay longer. They found a portable television set with a long cord and wheeled it in, and we watched it together, the way we would at home. Clearly he was on the mend.

He was doing so well that on the fifth day after surgery he was moved to a regular room. It felt like a five-star hotel compared to the ponderous array of equipment in Intensive Care. Sylvio spent the day doing his breathing exercises. He ate an apple, his first food in nine days. As I left that evening, he asked me to bring him a pack of cigarettes! I gave him the dirtiest scowl I could muster, but I took his interest as a sign that he was feeling more like himself again. I was happy.

That night I slept soundly for the first time. Relief enveloped me. Our ordeal was over! Sylvio was on his way home.

But my jubilation was to be short-lived. When I arrived the next morning, he had been hemorrhaging again. After a while, I realized that no one was doing anything about it. I went out to the public telephone in the corridor, dialed the hospital's regular outside phone number, and asked the operator to page the lung specialist. He picked up the page, and I told him what was going on.

He came to the room and began to act immediately. Within hours, Sylvio was being prepped for another emergency surgery.

As he was being wheeled into the Operating Room, he begged them not to operate. He pleaded with me to let him die. I didn't consider the possibility because I knew the hemorrhaging had to be stopped. He had been so well the day before, I fully believed that this was just one more hurdle that had to be dealt with. Once it was taken care of, he could come home.

When he came out of surgery, he was sent back to the ICU. Once again he was attached to the respirator and the other machines. Again his hands were tied down. He writhed in pain, alert to all that was going on and being said. This time he required constant transfusions.

He hadn't had food for ten days, except for the apple, and he was getting very weak. When I asked again about his having some nourishment, they said he was too wasted: there was concern that feeding him would fuel an infection.

Earlier I had called his sister Maria Selma in Brazil to tell her what was happening, and she decided to come right away. Sylvio was already back in the ICU by the time she arrived with her daughter Patrícia. They helped me tirelessly. A few days later his daughter Cláudia arrived, followed by his youngest daughter, Sylvia. Andréa decided not to come. I understood. She said she wanted to remember him the way he was the summer before, and I'm sure that's what Sylvio would have wanted, too. His daughters waited along with the rest of us. It was very hard for them to see their father in his condition, especially because they arrived after he could no longer talk.

Each day brought new problems. Stress ulcers in his stomach began to bleed, and medical students took turns irrigating his stomach with ice water for hours on end. Then he got pneumonia, which was treated and brought under control. His mouth developed sores from the respirator, so a breathing tube was surgically inserted in his windpipe. The bleeding from the ulcers continued. Blood was running through him so fast that it didn't have time to do the work that blood is supposed to do. He broke the record for the number of transfusions received by a single patient in the history of the unit. His kidneys began to fail.

Through it all, he was fully conscious, answering my questions with nods or shakes of the head and squeezes of the hand, and begging for relief with his eyes. There was no respite: no coma, no protective haze. Even sleep, when it came to him, was fitful.

Despite the doctors' reports and all that I was seeing, I still had hope. He had already had the strength to overcome numerous setbacks. I continued to make conversation and bring him news. His most recent book, on António Francisco Lisboa, was already at the printer's in Brazil. Another piece of news: he had been granted "amnesty"! He frowned. I knew he didn't want amnesty; what he wanted was an apology. If he could have talked, he would have said:

"Amnesty is for people who've done something wrong. They can keep their amnesty; I don't want it."

Nonetheless, I think at some level he knew it was a great relief for his family and friends in Brazil. Most important, he was now free to return.

The pulmonologist went away for five days. When he came back on March 10, he sat down with me and confided that the picture was much "bleaker" than when he left. He spoke of "multisystem failure." He explained to me patiently that when one of the body's systems fails, the others have some flexibility to compensate, and there is even hope of repairing the failing system over time. But when more than one system breaks down, hope fades significantly. The outlook is almost always poor. Later that day I saw the head of the ICU in the cafeteria, and he said:

"I think we should talk."

We never did.

By Tuesday, March 13, Sylvio had received 136 units of blood. He had had 63 bedside chest X-rays and 767 laboratory tests. His hospital bill was the size of a telephone book.

He suddenly got much worse. His 6-foot-4 frame had become an emaciated skeleton. His skin was dark yellow. Spontaneous sores were bleeding on his legs. His body was constantly writhing, arms and legs flailing out of control. His mouth, thickly rimmed with foam, was stretched wide open in the shape of a silent scream.

The shock of seeing him that way was almost unbearable. I felt his pain as if it were my own. And I felt utterly helpless. We had each spent the last nine years trying to make things right for the other. I had struggled for the last 20 days dealing with one challenge after another. Now I realized there was nothing in my power that would give him relief. I had run out of solutions.

He had told me on earlier occasions that both his father and his father's mother had had to be helped to die. Without asking me for a commitment, he implied that he hoped I would do the same thing for him if he was having a difficult death. He repeatedly asked me to promise not to use extraordinary measures to keep him alive. I remembered how he had pleaded with me not to go ahead with the second surgery.

Now he was in torment. His agony was tearing me apart. But I still couldn't accept that he was dying. It was too much for me to grasp. For at least a day his family had been convinced that we needed to intervene and slow down the efforts to keep him alive. Over the hours, as I watched and felt his suffering, I finally managed to understand that helping him to die was the only thing I had left to give him.

With Cláudia at my side, I approached the doctor in charge. It was the night shift. The regular head of the ICU had gone home, and his replacement was new to the case. I mumbled something vague about cutting back on Sylvio's treatments. The doctor was shocked. His eyes got as wide as saucers:

"We can't *do* that!" he said in horror.

He walked away abruptly.

I continued to consult with the family. By then we all agreed that Sylvio was suffering too much and that something had to be done. I had been counting on Dr. "Fish-Eyes" to discuss the options with us, but he hadn't been any help. It was up to us to make a proposal, and I didn't know enough about the treatment he was getting to be specific. Then the transfusions occurred to me. They didn't seem to be helping, and stopping them might make the end come a little sooner. On the other hand, the respirator seemed vital. Cláudia and I both felt it was too cruel, too final to cut off his breathing.

The doctor came back, and he seemed more open to discussion. It's possible that he had gone to look at Sylvio's chart and check his condition. I asked him about the transfusions: What would happen if they were discontinued, but the respirator was left on? Without predicting an outcome, he agreed to stop them.

The nurse on duty said that it would all be over shortly. Because Sylvio was so restless, she suggested that we bring in some music to calm him down. A young friend, Paulo, found a battery-operated tape player and some Brazilian music. Cláudia chose the songs. The player was set up in the room.

The ICU staff allowed us each to go in and see him one last time. We were not allowed to stay. One by one, everyone went in. I was the last. I took his hand and told him we had reached a decision and a solution was in sight. He nodded, acknowledging me with his eyes. I kissed him on the forehead. I couldn't bring myself to say good-bye.

Conflicts were tearing me apart. He wanted to be let go, and I couldn't watch him suffer any longer. Yet losing him was more than I could bear. I wanted him to live more than anything in the world, and part of me still hadn't given up. It was terrifying to think that he could die because of a decision I had made. My decision was mental, and my heart couldn't accept it.

The nurse drew the blinds on the windows and the door.

As I walked away, I could hear the music on the tape player. The song was the lilting refrain of a samba dancer who had run out of options: his girlfriend had left him, his money had run out, he had nowhere to go, and on top of it all, his shoe had worn through:

"Meu sapato já furouu . . ."

I would never see him again.

Part III

Grief and Guilt

11

SYLVIO DIDN'T DIE RIGHT AWAY. Though the doctor and nurses had told us that he would only live a short time without the transfusions, he defied their predictions and continued to struggle. We weren't allowed to see him. The wait seemed interminable and there was nothing we could do.

At first I couldn't feel any feelings at all, but my mind kept churning the same thoughts over and over again. "If only . . ." they would begin, and I would proceed to blame myself and the doctors for bad decisions that were made along the way. As Sylvio's time stretched out, I began to think he might have lived if we hadn't stopped the transfusions. I thought of asking the doctors to re-start them. But I didn't. I was torn all over again, and I didn't know what to do. Because I wasn't trying to save him, I believed that I was causing him to die. I was overcome with guilt.

We sat through the night and watched the sun rise the next morning. The regular head of the ICU came back on duty. He told me he was going to increase the dose of morphine and add some other drugs. Still, nothing happened.

Finally, just before noon, he came into the waiting room looking tired and sad and announced quietly:

"He's gone."

My first reaction was relief. His struggle had been so horrific.

Sylvio had given me a letter to be opened at the time of his death, and I had done that while we were waiting. In it, he said he did not want to be seen by his loved ones after he died. I showed his letter to the others.

The doctor asked if I wanted to see him. Respecting Sylvio's wish, I declined the offer. I have often wondered if seeing him would have given me more closure. I still dream that he's alive, more than thirty years later.

I was in a daze as I drove back to the house. Silence had taken the place of all the thoughts that had been racing through my mind. There was nothing left to think about, and it was too soon to feel. The expression "shell-shocked" came to mind. I felt I had survived an experience as intense as combat on a battlefield. What I had been through was far too overwhelming to let it be felt.

I had gone many hours without sleep, and I thought that getting some rest would make things easier—give me strength, and possibly put some padding around the experience I had just been through. But I could only sleep for a few minutes. I would wake up suddenly and be reminded all over again of the hell that was waiting for me in consciousness. It was impossible to sleep or shut out reality.

Keeping out the pain became all-consuming. I saw it as something "out there," waiting for a chance to get inside. The harder I tried to keep it *out*, the more it tried to get *in*. When I took a breath, I was sure I could feel it traveling down my windpipe into my lungs. Keeping out the pain meant keeping out everything. Letting in air and food became a conscious effort that I had to convince myself I had to make.

My world was a terrifying blur. The only thing I could think of was the image of Sylvio the last time I saw him, struggling to die. It was deeply burned in my memory, and it became a fixation. I had never seen anything so horrible, and some force kept compelling me to go back and relive it. Mixed in with that memory was my decision to hasten his death. I couldn't get rid of the idea that if it hadn't been for my intervention, he might have lived. In my mind, I had killed Sylvio, the person I loved beyond anything else in the world. When people approached me to tell me how sorry they were, I had to bite my tongue to keep from saying, "He didn't die; I killed him."

I went to the funeral home and signed the papers for his cremation. They had had to make special accommodations because he was so tall. The funeral director commented on Sylvio's height and good looks and said,

"You must have made a handsome couple."

For a nanosecond it felt nice to still think of us as a "handsome couple." Then I had to face reality all over again. Each time I was reminded, I felt as if I was experiencing the shock for the first time.

For his memorial service I chose St. Thomas' Parish, a short walk from our home. The church had once been a place of worship for presidents, including Franklin Roosevelt, but most of it had burned to the ground in August 1970. Now all that was left were the ruins of the altar; the footprint of the rest the church, which had been turned into a prayer labyrinth; and the Parish Hall, where our service was held. We were blessed with a warm spring day. The turnout was a surprise: in addition to our friends, there were a number of people I didn't know, especially from the Brazilian Embassy. Chauffeured limousines blocked traffic. At the service, José Neistein, director of the Brazilian-American Cultural Institute, and our friend Niles Bond delivered moving eulogies. After the service, people came back to the house for refreshments, and the crowd spilled out onto the sidewalk.

My mother went back to the country the next day. Cláudia and Sylvia returned to Brazil, taking Sylvio's ashes with them. Maria Selma and Patrícia stayed for another month, but eventually they left, too, and then I was alone. Mother predicted I would have more people in my life than I wanted, but that didn't happen. What I wanted was Sylvio, and no one else could fill the void. Seeing them only reminded me of what I didn't have. The times when I did want to connect, I didn't know how to send the right signals.

In Brazil, Sylvio's memory was honored in many ways. Although it seemed very far away, I was gratified, and I wished he could have known that he was still remembered. I started a scrapbook of clippings. The Belo Horizonte newspaper ran the news of his death on the front page, and a few days later it devoted an entire section to him, featuring his last column, numerous tributes and reminiscences, and a spread of photographs discovered in archives and personal albums. The School of Architecture declared a day of mourning and closed its doors. A soccer game in the stadium started with a minute of silence in his memory. He was the sole subject of the first issue of a new magazine. His name was given to a library, a gallery, and two streets. His books were republished. The one that went to press a few months earlier was enhanced with a posthumous foreword by noted author Otto Lara Resende. It was a critical success and quickly went through three printings.

I was gradually coming to realize that Sylvio and the fulfilling life we had shared were gone. Everything had changed in a single, brutal stroke, and I wasn't sure that I could ever recover from it.

I went through the motions of living, too frightened and tense to feel or have a real cry. I would shed a few tears, then quickly close down again. At my job, I continued to work half-time. I spent the afternoons on the research project that Sylvio and I had been working on when he died.

As summer approached, I began to prepare a retrospective show of Sylvio's pen-and-ink drawings at the Brazilian-American Cultural Institute. José, the director, graciously made the galleries available. I borrowed back the pieces that were already in the hands of private owners and prepared the rest of them for display and sale, save for a few that I had set aside as gifts to family and friends in Brazil. I wanted other people to have and enjoy them, and I knew that that's what Sylvio would have wanted. I taught myself how to make mats, cut glass, and assemble frames. I put my heart into it, and when the time came to hang the exhibit in July, every picture was framed. The opening drew a large crowd. Many drawings were sold, and the proceeds went toward purchasing a multi-volume encyclopedia for the Institute's library.

I also put together a selection of Sylvio's columns for publication. I organized his carbon copies of more then 300 manuscripts and solicited opinions from a small jury of friends and family. The book was published in Brazil under the title *Crônicas do Exílio*—Chronicles from Exile.[17]

In late August I returned to school. I thought the classes would give me structure and help keep me out of trouble. At least they would keep my mind busy. Registration in those days was chaotic. I used to say it was the hardest part of going to school; after that, the rest of the semester was easy. As usual, the huge gymnasium was filled with hundreds of people milling around, there were long lines, and loud voices were complaining about things that had gone wrong.

When I went to pay my tuition, I was told that my account showed a credit and I didn't owe any money. In fact, there was a large balance in my favor, enough to see me through two or three semesters. I felt sure it had to be a bookkeeping error, but it wasn't the time or place to look into it.

Still confused about the money, I moved on to the next station, where a lady handed me a form preprinted with my personal information and instructed me to update it if necessary. Sylvio's name was staring at me as my next of kin. I felt as if I had been kicked in the stomach: my wonderful partner, who always had my back, was no longer there for me! Worse yet, I was being forced to scratch him out. I couldn't control my feelings any longer. I sat down at an empty table and cried, oblivious to the noisy, milling stampede around me.

Then I suddenly thought: it must have been Sylvio who put the money in my account! I couldn't hold back any longer; I started to sob. Though I will never know for sure, the idea that Sylvio might have paid up my tuition in advance was enough to release the tension I had been holding onto. I went home and sobbed until I had no more tears.

I was finally able to open up to my grief.

As the months wore on, I lost a lot of weight. My clothes no longer fit. I had thought my grief would eventually pass, but it was only getting worse because I was finally allowing myself to feel it. Everything seemed more challenging than before.

I began to feel that I couldn't cope any longer, and I sought out a psychiatrist. I didn't take the decision lightly, but I felt that I could no longer handle the situation myself. Outside help was needed.

Dr. Bittelmann was a short man of German stock. He had fathered seven sons and raised them by a set of strict rules. He ran a tight ship and showed little sympathy as far as I could tell. He expected me to stop being emotional, shape up, and move on with my life. I walled myself off and built up resistance. I perceived him to be harsh and totally unfeeling. He shocked me with his sternness. As the weeks passed, he pointed out more than once that I was "holding on" to a man who was dead. That felt cruel because Sylvio's death was so recent and the wound was still very fresh to me.

Despite my discomfort with his rigid approach, I kept on seeing him. I took doctors seriously and wanted to be a "good patient." The idea of changing to another one didn't even occur to me.

I was overwhelmed with guilt about my clumsy intervention at the hospital and blaming myself for Sylvio's death. I needed to make sense of the unbearable idea that I had killed the person I loved the most. I was also aware, even then, that my feelings were an echo of a lifelong mix of loss and guilt. I wanted to talk about this, but Dr. Bittelmann dismissed my feelings. Surely I understood that the hospital would not have withheld treatment if Sylvio had had any chance of surviving. He seemed to think his logic was sufficient to put the case to rest. We never mentioned the subject again.

My real problem, Dr. Bittelmann said, was that I was angry at Sylvio for leaving me and wouldn't admit it because I was afraid to express anger. While that was not the analysis I expected, I dutifully accepted that I had to work on my anger because he said so. We discussed what to "do" with it, as if it were a force that could be released if I only knew how. I had to learn how to be angry. "Doing" something with anger meant bringing it out in the open.

I understood that I was supposed to start expressing my anger in everyday situations. I thought it was my mandate. Awkwardly, I sought to take a stand in situations where I was feeling upset. Later I learned that "taking a stand" requires great skill and works best precisely when one is not emotionally invested. At the time, however, my insecure, unpracticed attempts evoked responses that I didn't know how to handle, and some relationships were damaged beyond repair. One woman, a colleague at work, didn't speak to me for more than ten years. The fallout from these confrontations only added to my feelings of sadness, anxiety, and loneliness.

One of the specific targets of my anger that I could easily identify was the surgeon who said he found "rats and snakes" in Sylvio's chest. Days after Sylvio died, he sent me a bill for $2,285—typical for major surgery in the 1970s—and demanded payment within 30 days. I was deeply resentful of his crude manner after the surgery, his implication that Sylvio was responsible for his disease, and also the tone and bad timing of his letter. Moreover, a physician friend suggested that he had made a mistake and that his error had led to the second and fatal surgery. Much later I wondered if he might have felt some liability and was taking the offensive, making sure to collect his money in an effort to avoid being sued. I wrote him an over-the-top letter complaining about his demeanor (not mentioning his competence, because I didn't know for sure) and asking to pay the bill in installments. He responded by reiterating his demand for immediate payment. The situation dragged on until I finally paid the bill, leaving me even more upset and frustrated than ever.

In short, I was a complete failure at figuring out what to do with my anger. I wasn't the kind of person who could blow off steam by pounding a punching bag. My failed attempts convinced me that ventilating it made things worse for me instead of better. I realized that expressing it reinforced it. On top of that, I was creating a feedback loop with the people I was venting at, generating more anger on all sides.

Not long after that I read about the "antiventilationists," as they called themselves.[18] This was a movement of therapists and counselors who were taking issue with the "anger industry." So I wasn't the only one for whom venting didn't seem to work.

I eventually did learn how to deal with anger. I have several ways of nipping it in the bud. For example, when a feeling of anger comes up, I focus on the feeling, instead of my thoughts about it, and I simply stay with the feeling without reacting. The feeling usually goes away, and with it, the thoughts I had been having that triggered the anger in the first place. This is the opposite of "doing" something. It's not repressing or expressing or sublimating or neutralizing the feeling. It's simply releasing it before it gets a chance to take hold.

I recognize potential triggers and make a point of distracting myself before my feelings get carried away. Another technique is to reframe my thoughts in ways that don't make me feel angry or upset. I may also ask myself if I know that the conclusion I have reached is absolutely true. Or I may try to put myself in the other person's shoes.

I have also learned that the anger I feel about a situation today is often a proxy for deep anger from long ago. What I think I am steamed up about is seldom, if ever, the real story. I tell myself: if this anger isn't really about what I think it's about, then it's a waste of time and energy, and it only leads to trouble down the road.

But none of this was available to me three decades ago, and from what I understood, Dr. Bittelmann was only guiding me toward venting my anger. Still, I stuck with the therapy. I remembered what my first husband, John, the psychiatrist, had said:

"When things get tough, I make them tougher."

John's approach appeared to have worked with his patients, and I thought that perhaps I had to face even more challenges in order to put my current ones in perspective. Though I had many reservations about Dr. Bittelmann, I did credit him with some useful wisdom. I learned a lot about hanging in and tackling problems. His practical approach kept my feet on the ground when I might otherwise have ended up in a much more perilous place.

12

ONE THING WAS CERTAIN: LOGIC had failed to make any dent in my guilt. It didn't respond to reason, and my remorse and regret continued to intensify. As they did, feelings about my recent experience connected and merged with memories of similar struggles in the past. I began to dwell on a tragedy that occurred when I was six years old.

We were living in Larchmont, outside New York City. By that time, my father was largely out of the picture. Mother took me upstate to spend the summer at my grandparents' home in Rochester, where I had stayed many times before. We had moved around so much that I thought of Rochester as home. It was where we went back every year for Christmas. Mother was born in the same house, so it was also where I had roots. It represented security, and it was where I most liked to be.

The rambling Victorian structure was a time capsule from a bygone era. It had no electricity. Illumination came from gas sconces on the walls. Every evening my grandmother—I called her "Rosie"—would make her rounds and light the fixtures. In the kitchen, she had to use a hand pump next to the sink to get water. For hot water, she would put it in a pot and heat it on the coal-fired cook stove. The stove also heated the irons she used to press my clothes. Next to the kitchen was a back staircase that led to a secret bedroom under the eaves. The house fascinated me and I loved it exactly the way it was.

Out front, to the left of the main entrance, was a discreet brass plaque that said simply "Dr. Brown." It identified the office suite of my grandfather—the one who campaigned against unnecessary surgery—and its separate entrance for patients. Inside were a large waiting room, an office with a desk, and two examining rooms.

My grandparents didn't speak to each other. It had been that way for as long as I ever knew. One of the examining rooms had been turned into a bedroom, and Grandfather lived in his office suite. He was in his early seventies, and his practice had dwindled, so the waiting room became his parlor where he received visitors. Rosie would leave his meals on a tray at a door behind the stairs. She would tap lightly and announce in a sing-song voice:

"WILLiam, your dinner is here!"

. . . or breakfast or lunch, depending on the meal. A few minutes later he would open the door and pick it up. That was the extent of their communication. She was holding a grudge against him for some reason and often referred to him as a "beast."

Despite this arrangement, and Rosie's efforts to discredit him, I loved him very much. He was more of a father to me than my own father, and I certainly spent a lot more time with him. I would knock on his door and he would unlock it and let me in. We would talk or play games, or, if he was working at his rolltop desk, he would hold me in his lap. Sometimes he would sing to me. My favorite was "There is a tavern in the town . . ." He smelled like tar, from a cream he applied to large red patches that covered his face and arms. I didn't mind the smell or his appearance. He explained that his condition was called *psoriasis*.

I told him I wanted a dollhouse more than anything in the world. Inspired by the Rochester house, I had managed to acquire a small collection of Victorian miniatures. It had started with a replica of the cook stove in Rosie's kitchen, with movable parts no less, and already included a clawfoot bathtub, a pull-chain toilet and pedestal wash basin, a rope bed and matching bureau with sliding drawers, and a tilt-top table. I spurned the crude furniture seen in ordinary dollhouses. I'm a stickler when it comes to aesthetic details, and that trait had already emerged.

One day Grandfather announced he was going to make me the dollhouse that I wanted so badly. I was overjoyed. He got hold of some plywood and set up sawhorses in the back yard. The next morning I went out to check on his progress. He had already put together three sides and a pitched roof, and he had cut holes for the front door and the windows above it. The problem was that the windows were almost three times the size of the door. They were way out of proportion, and I could see that they would never work. I also realized immediately that it was too late—he couldn't go back and make the holes smaller.

I told him outright that the windows were too big. He hesitated for a moment and then rationalized:

"I did that on purpose, so your dolls can lean out and see who's at the front door."

He used his hands to show me how it was supposed to work. I wasn't buying his explanation. In fact, I felt insulted that he expected me to settle for such a lame excuse. We had a brief exchange, and then he seemed to recognize that the situation was hopeless. To please me, he would have had to start all over.

We stared at each other. He looked crushed. His posture suddenly stiffened and his eyes opened wide. Without a word, he turned his back, walked inside the house, and killed himself.

I was not to know the facts until decades later, but I understood instantly that something terrible had happened and it was my fault. At lunchtime, Rosie left his tray at the door, and he didn't pick it up. She tried all the doors, but they were locked, as usual. As the afternoon wore on, she started knocking louder and calling his name over and over again. Uncle Neil—Mother's brother who lived in Rochester—arrived and managed to open the door behind the stairs. When he came back out, his face was ashen and he said something to Rosie in a whisper.

She quickly ushered me into the sunroom, drew the shades, and closed the doors. From inside my dark cell I heard sirens, men trooping in and out of the house, loud voices, more people coming and going, muted voices, whispered conversations. Silences. Then more whispered conversations. These confusing events went on long into the evening. I remember feeling very frightened. I knew that something had happened to Grandfather, and I knew I had done something terribly wrong. I needed to understand what was going on, but I had been abandoned and ignored, as if I didn't exist. As an adult, I have often felt that I would rather know anything, no matter what, than tolerate the anxiety of *not* knowing. Those hours inside the dark room may have been the first time I was aware of that feeling.

In the morning, I found Uncle Neil out front taking down Grandfather's "shingle"—the brass plaque that said "Dr. Brown." I asked him where Grandfather was.

"He's gone on a trip."

Skeptical, I probed:

"So when is he going to finish my dollhouse?"

I figured that if Grandfather was working on the dollhouse, it would mean that all was forgiven from the day before. Also, an answer to the dollhouse question might tell me where he was.

He responded dismissively:

"*You* don't need a dollhouse. You're too *old* for a dollhouse."

I couldn't believe that Grandfather had gone on a trip, and I hated that Uncle Neil was trying to talk me into something that didn't make sense—just like Grandfather had done. But I gave up. He knew something I didn't know, and he wasn't telling me.

Mother arrived that evening. I asked *her* about my dollhouse, reporting what Uncle Neil had said. Her answers weren't any more informative. The next morning after breakfast she led me out to the gazebo in the garden, sat down, and took me in her lap. She explained to me that Grandfather wouldn't be able to finish the dollhouse because he had died from a sudden heart attack. I cried. I felt really sad, but I was also worried and scared, because I knew that whatever had happened to him, I had caused it. I couldn't tell her—or anyone else. I would not learn that he committed suicide until I was a grown woman, but I knew enough to blame myself for his death.

·

There was no funeral. He was quietly buried in his home town of Penfield, a few miles east of Rochester. According to his obituary in the *Journal of the American Medical Association*, he died of "illuminating gas poisoning, self administered."[19] In other words, he had turned on a gas light fixture without igniting the flame.

Mother took me home on the train, and I never saw the house again. It was torn down. Not only had I killed Grandfather, who had been the closest I ever had to a real father, but I had also killed the house—my roots, my beloved heritage.

I became incommunicative and only spoke when I had to. The silence went on for a year, and Mother was worried about me.

Aunt Muriel, ever the well-intentioned psychologist, thought she could cure my silence by taking me on a trip. The next summer, she and I took off on a six-week adventure in her Ford Coupé. She was teaching a summer course at the college in Fort Collins, Colorado, and she filled up my time with lessons, including swimming.

One day I was taken with a group of children to a public pool. I was playing with some of the kids in shallow water when the lifeguard started shouting and blowing his whistle. We were herded out of the water and into a bath house that was totally dark inside. The other kids and I took turns peeking through a crack to see what was happening. I felt both frightened and compelled to watch. I saw the lifeguard pull a boy's body out of the water and start to give him artificial respiration. Soon an ambulance arrived. The medics worked for a long time trying to revive him—it seemed interminable. Eventually they gave up and pronounced him dead.

I saw his mother when she realized he couldn't be saved: she started screaming and lurching convulsively as two men grabbed her and struggled to restrain her. I could feel her raw, unimaginable grief. Even looking back today, the image in my memory overwhelms me.

As I recalled the events in the pool, I thought I remembered a blurred form on the bottom near where I had been playing. Forcing myself to reconstruct what happened, I became convinced that I had been near the boy before he drowned. I even thought that I might have pushed him down in the water. I pieced together a scenario in my mind, but the memories were vague and fuzzy. It wasn't at all like my crystal-clear recollection of the events in Rochester, but nonetheless I chose to take responsibility for the boy's death and incorporate it into the burden I was already carrying.

When I got back to Larchmont, Mother saw that my silence was even deeper than when I left. She had the idea to get me a kitten. I named him "Spooks," because his markings reminded me of a spooky pattern of shadows. I played with him and cuddled him, but I rarely talked. After a couple of weeks, Spooks got sick. We thought he had turned the corner. However, just when things were looking up, I came home from school one day and found him lying dead on his pillow, surrounded by dark feces. I let out a shriek. I phoned Mother at work, and she came home as quickly as she could. I sobbed and sobbed in her arms. It was the release I needed, and I started to open up. My voice returned. I told her about the boy in the pool. But I never told her about my last conversation with Grandfather. I was too ashamed.

As I got on with the business of growing up, the Rochester story and the boy in the pool were relegated to the background. I rarely thought about them. But I was quick to assume blame and punish myself for anything that went wrong. I consistently overreacted.

13

G UILT WAS PAINFUL, YET, LIKE a moth to the flame, I kept reinforcing it. It had different nuances. There was remorse over my missteps. There was regret that I couldn't turn back the clock and create different outcomes. And there was always deep shame. The pattern continued into adulthood.

When I was 25, I got pregnant. It wasn't an accident. I wanted to have a baby. I went to see a doctor who was a personal friend, and when the test came back positive, I was elated. I was so excited that I was oblivious to the consequences. It was as if my desire for motherhood had numbed my powers of reason. The reality was that I wasn't married and I hadn't given a single thought to how I was going to manage a new life with a child to take care of.

Back in the 1950s, it was shocking for an unmarried woman to have a baby. Once her belly began to show, she was expected to go into hiding. If she was in school, she was expelled; if she was working, her boss had to fire her.[20] There were "homes for unwed mothers" where she could spend the last months of her pregnancy out of sight. The alternative was to move to another city, make up a story, and live a lie. If people found out, the child was stigmatized for life. Regardless of how she handled her pregnancy, she faced both social and financial challenges after her child was born. And getting by on a woman's wages with the added cost of raising a child was more than most young women could handle.

I knew all that, but somehow it didn't sink in. Had I looked at my situation objectively, I would have realized that I was facing gigantic roadblocks. I was working as a secretary on a salary of $325 a month while trying to earn a bachelor's degree in my spare time. My lover of four years, much older than me, was still married. Though he had been separated from his wife for a long time and his kids were grown, he was Catholic and didn't believe in divorce.

Getting pregnant was never a ploy to get him to marry me. In my saner moments, I knew the relationship was toxic. He was obsessed with himself and had a hideous temper that he made no effort to control. In the evenings he drank gin and it intensified his rage exponentially. I would watch his face distort as his anger rose in increments. He would rant and bellow for hours on end. Sometimes his fury was directed at me, and my insides would churn with fear and self-recrimination. If it was directed toward someone else, I would get bored and start thinking that the relationship was a bad idea.

Still, once I was pregnant, a part of me wished he would get a quick divorce and at least make my baby "legitimate"—though I knew it wasn't likely to happen. Another option was a marriage of convenience to someone else, which I actually did consider. Regardless of whether or not I had a husband and a new surname for the child, I was sure that I could manage as a single mother and keep on working. I figured, if things didn't pan out in Washington, I would move somewhere else. However, these thoughts were just loose scenarios bouncing around in my head. The fact is, I had no real plan. Giving up the child never crossed my mind.

My lover's mind, on the other hand, was running on an entirely different track. He was a well-known figure on the Washington scene, and his career and reputation were his top priority. A baby would cause a scandal. He told me to "take care of it." Period. I knew what he meant, and the idea was more than repugnant to me. I vehemently resisted his suggestion. I vowed that no one would find out; his reputation would be safe. We would argue about it, then let the subject drop. Then argue again. Days stretched into weeks, and nothing got resolved. A doctor examined me and declared that I was at least 14 weeks pregnant. He advised me to have the baby and give it up for adoption.

As my belly started to show, my confidence began to waver. Back then, it was much harder for a woman to stand up to a man, let alone strike out on her own. It became clear that getting married in the next few months was not in the cards, and I was beginning to understand the challenges of raising a baby as a single mother. My lover, for his part, had started to panic and was putting pressure on me to end the pregnancy.

In those days, abortion was a crime throughout the United States. Doctors who performed the procedure were subject to severe punishment, and their reputation was endangered if they helped a woman who had had an abortion. The women were shamed and harassed. Back-alley abortions were highly unsafe, if not fatal. The "solution" was to go to a foreign country. The luxury destinations were in Europe. However, my lover did his own research and surprised me one day with a plane ticket to Havana, Cuba. He informed me that I had an appointment with a doctor there. The envelope also included several thousand dollars in cash to cover the doctor's fee. I felt powerless to continue defending my unrealistic position. It seemed as if I had run out of options. I no longer had a choice.

I got on the plane with a heavy heart. The money was stuffed in a belt around my already bulging waist. By then I estimated that I was about 16 weeks pregnant.

Havana felt warm and steamy compared with the late January cold of Washington. Fidel Castro had marched into the city and taken over the government just weeks before I arrived. The people who arranged my trip were unaware of the implications. One of the new government's first acts was to outlaw abortion.

I managed to get through Immigration and change some money without a problem. I was clutching a phone number that I was supposed to call on arrival. My instructions were to place the call from the public phones in the concourse, which I did. The doctor himself answered, speaking in labored English until I reassured him that I understood Spanish. In essence, he said:

"The airport is dangerous. Don't speak to anyone! Most important: stay away from the taxis at the exit. Don't say a word to the drivers!"

Instead, he told me to walk down the hill to the main road toward town, hail a cab that wasn't coming from the airport, and ask to be taken to the address that he then proceeded to dictate to me. In closing, he repeated:

"Remember, do not speak to anyone!"

As I walked away from the phone, before I even had a chance to digest my instructions, a tall, burly man in a suit came up and asked me tauntingly in English:

"Hey, Lady! Did you come to see the doctor?"

Had he overheard the conversation? Was my belly showing that much? I got scared. Something was going on that no one had told me about. Without knowing why, I was afraid I could be in serious trouble. I started walking, and the man proceeded to follow me. I walked faster and I felt my adrenaline rising. The hack stand was directly in front of the exit; I couldn't avoid it. The man, now right behind me, said something to the dispatcher, and the drivers surrounded me, trying everything short of force to get me inside one of their cabs.

I kept on walking, my eyes riveted ahead. The man in the suit followed me down to the main road and then gave up. I managed to hail a passing cab and breathed a huge sigh of relief as I settled into the back seat and gave the address to the driver.

My destination turned out to be a small hotel in the suburbs. The front desk was expecting me. I checked in and called the doctor again from my room. He came and picked me up in his personal car and we drove to a residential apartment complex. One of the apartments, bearing no indication that it was a doctor's office, turned out to be a small medical suite with a rudimentary treatment room. A nurse was waiting. The doctor was relieved that I spoke Spanish, which meant that he didn't have to hire an interpreter.

On examination, he found that my pregnancy was more advanced than I had said, and he was both concerned and annoyed. He asked me to confirm that I wanted him to proceed. For a brief moment I was elated to have an excuse not to go through with it. Then I thought of all that had happened and the consequences that would face me. I had made the decision against everything I wanted or believed in, and I had just survived the long and dangerous trip to get there. Reversing the momentum seemed overwhelming. I envisioned my lover's rage and thought of the challenges I had become aware of in recent weeks. I didn't see any alternative. With my heart breaking, I told him to go ahead. I have often relived those last moments when I still had a chance to change my mind.

The nurse gave me ether, but much of the time I wasn't really asleep. I felt the pain and had wild, vivid dreams. I was also aware of the conversation between the two of them and I heard a toilet flush more than once. When it was over, he told me I had been carrying a boy. When I was able to stand on my feet, he led me to the toilet and pointed to the remaining dismembered parts of my baby floating in blood. I will never forget what I saw. He flushed the toilet again, and as I watched, the last pieces of my child washed down to the sewer like common waste.

My return to Washington was endless. The flight to Miami was commandeered by disheveled armed troops and diverted to a small airport in the midst of cane fields on the eastern part of the island. There were about ten passengers, and we were made to wait in a bunker-like building for what seemed like an eternity. By that time I was convinced I had committed a crime, and I wondered if the soldiers were after me. However, my fears proved to be unfounded. Eventually we were led back to the plane and it was allowed to resume the trip.

By the time we reached Miami, not only had I missed my connection, but flights had been cancelled because of winter weather in the north. A crowd had gathered on the tarmac. As I stood waiting, I realized that blood was streaming down my legs and pooling inside my shoes. I was biting my lip to keep from passing out, and I was afraid to ask for help.

When I finally arrived in Washington, my lover was waiting for me in one of his usual rages. My delay had upset his social calendar:

"You always mess things up, don't you? Right now I'm supposed to be at a formal dinner at the Chinese Embassy. No thanks to you, there's an empty seat at the table."

I was extremely weak. He took me to my apartment and I fell into bed, barely conscious. The doctor friend who had done the pregnancy test back in the beginning came to check me out, but he was afraid to do anything for fear of getting in trouble. He just sat by my bed and forced me to stay awake and keep drinking water to replace the blood I was losing. He and my lover waited through the night to make sure my condition was stabilized. They were both afraid—more for themselves than for me.

For weeks I could think of nothing but my baby. The grief and remorse were more than I could bear. I began to sob uncontrollably, to the point that I could no longer function. Friends and family intervened, and the doctors declared I was having a "nervous breakdown." Before long I found myself in a ward for mental patients, where I was given a long series of electroshock treatments. I came out with almost no memory of the events of the past year, and it took many more years for my memory to return. I couldn't work, and for months I didn't even recognize my friends. I did remember feeling stripped of my identity in the locked ward, and I remembered my baby in the toilet. The treatments took a heavy toll, but they never erased the cause of my emotional pain.

I broke up with my lover because I could no longer stand the sight of him. In the end, word of the "scandal" leaked out and he lost his job anyway.

This memory, along with the ones from my childhood, flooded back to me in 1979 as I struggled with the belief that I had killed Sylvio. In daytime, logic and my ordinary routine prevailed, and I somehow managed to keep on going and do the things that were expected of me. At night, however, my demons took over and I had recurring dreams of my grandfather, my baby, and Sylvio in his last hours. I was being condemned for the deaths of all of them. Sometimes it was a panel of judges in a courtroom; other times it was a mob of people shouting at me, shaking their fists in the air. Or I would be trying to revive a dead baby. The message was always the same: I was a murderer, and I had killed the ones I loved the most. The idea was stuck in my soul, and there were enough fragments of reality to perpetuate and reinforce it.

14

SIX MONTHS AFTER SYLVIO'S DEATH I was still struggling with remorse and guilt. What had changed was that I was able to express my grief. After I finally broke down, it became easy to cry. Until then, I had focused on trying *not* to feel my emotions. Now, wherever I went, the slightest reminder of him would start me off. Old people on the street made me cry—it wasn't fair that they were still here and he wasn't. Music made me cry. Every evoked memory made me cry. In Portuguese class, a reference to Coimbra reminded me of our trip to Portugal and I had to leave the room.

Christmas was approaching, and I dreaded the prospect of getting through the holidays without Sylvio. To escape the many reminders that would bring up memories, I invited myself to spend two weeks with my cousin Trine and her family in Norway—my father's country of birth. Not only did they welcome me graciously, they made me feel loved.

Their home was high up on a hill overlooking Oslo. The city stretched out below, all the way to the sea, and pine-covered hills surrounded its perimeter. Tiny white holiday lights twinkled their magic everywhere. The peaked roofs of old-style wooden structures snuggled comfortably under a plump white blanket. Snow fell softly almost every day, piling more on top of the trees' already fleecy coats and covering up tracks from the day before. A cross-country trail passing directly behind the house invited me to try out a pair of my cousin's skis. I got the knack of it quickly and was told that skiing appeared to be in my genes. Trine and I took the train to Bergen, and there I got to meet more of my relatives and see the house overlooking a fjord where my father was born. We visited our grandparents' gravesite in a small churchyard and took rubbings from the tombstones.

In addition to making cherished memories from these and other adventures, I learned a lot from Trine and her husband Tor. They were into personal growth and alternative approaches to healing. Trine was a homeopathic patient. She and Tor both belonged to support groups. He was in a drum circle. They were taking classes to learn how to play. For me, this was a new world. Back in Washington, I might not have paid much attention, but there in Norway, far from my problems and in such a caring environment, I became an eager student. We had many long conversations, and the topics fascinated me. I think of my time with them, and the interests that I inherited from it, as the first chink in the armor I had encased myself in for most of my life.

When I returned, physical problems started to emerge and compete for my attention. The first was a persistent pain deep in my throat. I started to look for someone who could diagnose what was going on. I went through several doctors until I finally found one who would listen to me. He was an eye, ear, nose, and throat specialist, and he seemed to think I had a problem worth studying. He ordered several tests to be done on an outpatient basis and two that required hospitalization—a scope of my esophagus and another of my windpipe and bronchi.

What was supposed to be a same-day affair kept me in the hospital for two days with complications. In his office the following week, the doctor told me that the lab tests had not revealed any problems. I was glad that he had at least taken an interest. I moved on, though the pain was still there.

As it happened, five years later I received a circular letter from the same doctor informing his patients that he was closing his practice. He offered to send a copy of my records, and I took him up on it. In his report of the in-hospital procedures, he confessed that the wrong kind of water had been used for the bronchial "washings"[21] and admitted that the error had probably damaged the cells being collected for study.[22] Referring to the scope of the esophagus, he reported "a thickened area . . . 17 cm down" and said that he removed a piece of tissue for biopsy.[23] I immediately looked for the report from the lab. When I read it, I couldn't decide whether to laugh or cry: the container submitted for biopsy was empty! He had lost the specimen. In other words, both procedures had been bungled, and my time and patience had been wasted.

February 1980 brought the anniversary of Sylvio's illness. The trip to Norway had worked so well, I decided to go to Brazil to mark the end of my first year without him. Though I was often told that I spoke Portuguese like a native, I had never been to Brazil. Sylvio had never had a chance to go back because his amnesty came only days before he died.

His family and friends welcomed me with open arms and went out of their way to show me a good time. In Rio de Janeiro, I stayed in three different homes and took in Sugarloaf, Christ the Redeemer, Copacabana, and many other beautiful parts of the city. On a Sunday, friends took me to spend a day at the country estate of Roberto Burle Marx, the famous artist and landscape designer, who had known Sylvio. I left with one of his original drawings, which he signed and dedicated to me. It is one of my prized possessions. In Sylvio's home state, Minas Gerais, I saw many of his friends and visited Ouro Preto and other colonial towns. The real purpose of my trip had been to visit Sylvio's grave. His ashes were buried in a cemetery in Belo Horizonte. I was able to find the location and spend an hour sitting next to him—talking, thinking, and just being with him on the anniversary of his death.

Since then I have returned to Brazil a number of times, recognizing that if I can't have Sylvio, being in his country helps to fill the void.

A few days after I got back, my handbag was stolen. Among other things, it contained my entire collection of snapshots of

Sylvio, which I had taken to show his family and friends. I was also carrying several pieces of gold jewelry that I had taken to have mended in Brazil.

Arriving home after a half day at work, I had dropped the bag on a chair and left the front door open while I went to the kitchen. Sunshine started to bark, and I heard strange noises in the living room. I rushed to see what was going on, but by the time I got there it was too late. I looked out the door and saw the thieves, two young boys, walking away, swinging their trophy in the air. Sunshine and I ran after them. Just as I was catching up, the younger one took the bag and ducked into an alley while the older one stood me off. I begged him:

"Pleeeease give it back! Those are they only pictures I have of my husband!"

He laughed: "Yeah, sure. I'll send your stuff back. I'll put it in the mail."

Of course he never did.

The whole episode was over in less than five minutes. In that short space of time, I lost not only my keys, passport, the usual things that one carries, the jewelry, and a handmade leather bag that I liked a lot, but also photos that were irreplaceable. A week later a street cleaner found my driver's license and checkbook in a gutter about a mile away. By then I had replaced what I needed to, but the photos and jewelry were gone. I felt violated, kicked, and beaten.

Shortly afterwards, I developed pain in my ribs. I mentioned it to Dr. Laird during a regular checkup, and he gave me a prescription for Vicodin, assuring me that it wouldn't be habit-forming. I wasn't so much interested in relieving the pain; I wanted to know what was causing it. I tore up the prescription.

The pain persisted, and I was having trouble breathing as well. I saw a lung specialist, who told me I had damage to my lungs which he termed "radiation fibrosis." It was a delayed side effect of the radiation therapy after my mastectomy. The damage was likely to be permanent, he said, and there was no treatment for it. He predicted that my lungs would get worse as I got older—which has turned out to be true. He added that the pain in my ribs could be chondritis—in other words, inflammation of the cartilage—and suggested that that, too, might also be an effect of the radiation.

Later I found out that all the problems I had been having—the thickening 17 cm down my throat, the inflammation around my ribs, and the situation in my lungs—were well recognized side effects of radiation. While the first two symptoms healed themselves, I later discovered in a book on the side effects of radiation therapy[24] that the damage to my lungs was not trivial. Though I didn't need convincing, there was more evidence than ever that I had received too much radiation.

Part IV

Round Two

15

By September 1980 I had developed a pain in my hip that made it difficult to walk. I also felt a stabbing pain in the groin and mentioned it to my gynecologist. To my surprise, he ordered a bone scan. I couldn't understand why, because the pain wasn't near a bone. The report that came back was a shock:

> The bone scan demonstrates a well-defined lesion in the right lateral margin of the 5th lumbar vertebra.
>
> The most likely etiology would be **metastatic disease.** If there is any clinical question, a bone biopsy may be useful.

Metastatic disease! The words jumped out at me from the page. They looked technical and impersonal, but I felt their force. I knew instantly that they had the power to change the rest of my life. I felt certain that my cancer had spread and I was going to die. A storm of mixed emotions came over me: fear, panic, helplessness, and, at the same time, a sense of resignation—even relief. After Sylvio died, there were times when I thought that dying would be easier than the struggle to keep on going. Now I had permission to give up. I didn't have to decide whether or not I wanted to die. The decision had been made for me. I had something *real* to think about. It was a distraction from the endless tapes that kept replaying inside my head.

My mind shifted into high gear. I wanted to know more. There's a big part of me that feels compelled to search for answers. It's probably my way of dealing with fear. The process of searching gives me a sense of security, regardless of the answers I find. I soon confirmed that when breast cancer has spread to the bones, patients usually die from their disease.[25]

At home that evening, I immediately phoned my friend Gladys in New York. Gladys had breast cancer and, like me, she also knew she had a lump but didn't get a diagnosis for nine months. Her delay was related to a job change. If her new employer had known about her lump, she wouldn't have gotten the job. Once she was hired, her new health plan had a six-month waiting period for pre-existing conditions, which added to her delay. Her predicament reminded me of my own challenges and the dream job that I lost because of health insurance. When Gladys finally did see a doctor, it turned out that she had two different tumors, and one of them was especially aggressive. Her cancer had already spread to the pelvic bone. The doctors gave her three years to live.

In our conversation that day, we joked about what it felt like to be a "goner," and we wondered what one actually dies from. Neither of us knew. That night I was afraid to fall asleep for fear I wouldn't wake up. I worried that I still had business to take care of.

I saw Dr. Laird a few days later. Based on the report from the scan, he made a presumptive diagnosis of "breast cancer metastasized to the spine." The lesion on the L5 vertebra would account for the pains in both my hip and groin, referred through nerve pathways. He went on to say that it is common for breast cancer to spread, and difficult to predict when it will. This was the same Dr. Laird who had been so encouraging about my outlook at the beginning. When I pointed out that it had been almost four years since my surgery, he said the time lapse can be ten, twenty, or even thirty years. He also explained that "cure" rates refer only to local recurrence of the original tumor in the breast itself. In other words, one could be "cured" and still die of spread to another site.

I felt that he had misled me about the seriousness of my original tumor in the breast. Considering its size, not only had it been growing for many years, but it had to have at least doubled in size while I waited for the diagnosis and was more than likely to have spread. Once it had spread to the bones, I had a high probability of dying from my disease.[26]

Ending on an optimistic note, he told me that my tumor had been tested for estrogen receptors in 1977 and was "mildly positive." It might be possible to treat me with "the new mega-hormones." He ordered hormone studies and a CEA test. [27] At the time, the CEA was used to gauge the body's attempt to fight off breast cancer. He also arranged for me to see the head of the oncology clinic at the hospital. The test results would be sent to him.

I learned much later that Dr. Laird thought I only had months to live.

My first response was to put my life on hold. I went straight to the registrar's office at school and withdrew from my classes. My disease was going to have my full time and attention. When I got home, I sat down and started a journal. It would be important to have a record of my thoughts and feelings as I moved along my path—a path that I was certain was leading to my death.

My next step was to see my lawyer and ask him to draw up a will. When I told him I had breast cancer, he said:

"Oh, you'll be fine. You don't have to worry until it spreads to the bones."

He proceeded to tell me about a client who had survived with breast cancer for a long time. She didn't die until it finally went to her bones.

Ouch! I told him that my disease had done just that. Though he had meant to encourage me, his offhand remark reinforced my pessimism.

Then I spoke with my friend Mark, who had reached out to me after Sylvio died. He came by to see me, but he didn't seem interested in the medical details I was sharing with him. When I paused to take a breath, he asked me, with a wisdom I could not appreciate at the time:

"Does it help you to know all this?"

I felt insulted and stopped talking. After an awkward silence, he confessed that he wasn't comfortable with people who were sick. Now that I was "sick," he didn't know what to say to me anymore. He left, and I felt lonelier and more abandoned than ever. From then on, our communication was formal and distant.

At the oncology clinic, the doctor went over the results of the tests and explained that the bone scan by itself was not conclusive. However, when combined with the high CEA count, the two together strongly suggested metastases. Just to be sure there hadn't been a false reading, he ordered a repeat of the CEA test. He also requested further tests and additional X-rays and scans "to get a better look" at the lesion in my spine. He said he hoped it would be possible to avoid a bone biopsy, since the spot was difficult to get to.

As for treatment, he said he was thinking of a combination of radiation and hormones. He also mentioned removal of my ovaries. While he was quite sure that the lesion in my spine was cancerous, he also seemed confident that the process was slow and urgent measures were not required.

I left feeling more disappointed than encouraged. Though the doctor had offered a plan, it wasn't what I expected. It seemed logical to me to do a biopsy—after all, it was a biopsy that confirmed my diagnosis four years earlier. Dr. Laird said that the only real diagnosis is the one that can be seen under a microscope. But the oncologist was against it. He had mentioned radiation, and I was afraid of it. I wasn't keen on having my ovaries removed, either. Moreover, his unhurried attitude left me hanging nervously. I remembered the delays back in 1976, and this time I wanted action—even though none of the options appealed to me.

That night I woke up in a cold sweat remembering that the doctor had mentioned radiation. My nights were like that. I would often wake up in a panic at around four o'clock, reminded of thoughts I had managed to put out of my mind during the day.

Whatever it was, it was magnified many times over in the middle of the night.

Cancer took over my conscious mind as well. Soon it was occupying my attention around the clock as I continued to ask myself questions and then look for the answers. I persuaded myself that my thoughts were constructive: learning the answers was preparing me to deal with the problem and make the right decisions. I didn't understand that, on the contrary, the constant focus was giving more power to cancer.

Long phone conversations with Gladys, my fellow cancer sufferer, became a Saturday afternoon ritual. We spent hours talking about the illness we shared in common. We were both lonely, despite our busy lives, and we were both obsessed with breast cancer. Gladys was an economist by profession and a consummate researcher. She collected her data and measured her progress in every detail: CEA levels, leukocyte counts, bone scans, and so on. Each new number went into her mental spreadsheet, and she would process it to the nth degree.

When I told her that the doctor at the clinic was still undecided about my diagnosis, she urged me to find an oncologist in private practice. That was her arrangement; she liked her doctor and felt motivated to work with him.

Shortly afterwards, I went back to the clinic to learn the results of my blood tests and X-rays. This time I was directed to a different waiting room. It was large and dingy, and so full that people were standing—more than twenty in all. I had to take a number from a machine and wait my turn. The apparatus was the old-fashioned kind: a big number on the wall was flipped with a chain as each person was called. It reminded me of waiting in line for the butcher as a child, and I began to feel like a piece of meat myself. The other people looked sad and vacant. Most of them were gaunt and had a greenish-gray pallor. Some seemed barely alive. Their despair gradually infected me as I sat among them.

It turned out that the doctor wasn't in the office and my two-hour wait had been for naught. Gladys was right: it was time for a change. I arranged to see Dr. Purcell, an oncologist in private practice. When I stopped by the clinic to pick up my records, I knew I had made the right decision. The stack of unfiled reports was three weeks old. Apparently none of them had been seen by a doctor. My most recent CEA test wasn't even there. The office had to call the lab and ask for the results over the phone.

My newest CEA level was even higher than the first. The special X-ray studies concluded that the lesion in my spine was due to a slow-growing ("sclerotic") process that was likely to be cancer. This process went beyond the vertebra itself and also showed up in a separate place on the tailbone.[28]

My mind was buzzing with questions for Dr. Purcell. How certain was the diagnosis? What was the problem with biopsying the bone? Could radiation be avoided? How well do the new hormone drugs work? Would my ovaries have to be removed? Were there experimental drugs that I could try?

To my surprise, Dr. Purcell didn't see the diagnosis as a sure thing. He wanted time to put the pieces together, especially before deciding on a bone biopsy. That was not exactly what I wanted to hear. I was hoping for answers, even if I didn't like the solutions.

After reviewing my history and talking with me for a bit, he leaned back in his chair and asked:

"Do *you* think you have cancer?"

"I'm not sure," I said, "but I feel that something strange is going on in my body."

That wasn't quite honest. The truth was, I was convinced that my cancer had spread.

"How urgently do you have to have an answer?"

I admitted that I wanted to know as soon as possible, but to give him the impression that I was wise and sensible, I said I also realized it was important for him to have time to make the right decisions.

When I asked him about experimental drugs, he said:

"You can forget about those. The protocols are almost impossible to qualify for. You have to meet very specific conditions—like purple stuff coming out of your nose every other Tuesday."

I got the point.

In concluding the visit, he said:

"The main thing is, you don't want this to become the centerpiece of your life."

His phrase struck a chord, because I realized that it already *was* the centerpiece of my life.

A few days later I went to see the oncologist at the clinic to tell him I was changing doctors. More important, he was going to go over the results of the tests. I was anxious to know his opinion, especially now that Dr. Purcell seemed unsure.

Consulting my chart, he said the results showed that I was a candidate for hormone therapy—in other words, treatment with the new drug tamoxifen.[29] He also thought I should have radiation. Other sites might appear later, and decisions about how to treat them could be made at that time. He added that radiation will not destroy a lesion in the bone once it's established; it only stops it from growing.

"You will have this lesion for the rest of your life," he said.

I asked him how sure he was that my cancer had spread, and he replied:

"Eighty-five percent."

That was enough to convince me. Despite Dr. Purcell's hesitation, there was no longer any doubt in my mind.

16

THE ONCOLOGIST'S "85 PERCENT" CONCLUSION that my cancer had spread gave me permission to feel morbid. I spent a lot of time thinking about whether or not I was going to die. After Sylvio's death, there were many times when death seemed welcome. After the first bone scan, I was certain that it was imminent. Now, with the diagnosis not fully confirmed, the imminent had gotten postponed. Nevertheless, the subject was as much on my mind as ever. The difference was that before I had had feelings about it; now it was a mental exercise. My anxiety dissipated as I got involved in the details. Thinking about it protected me from the rawness of its reality. I went out and bought *On Death and Dying*[30] by Elizabeth Kübler-Ross and ruminated about the subject for pages and pages in my journal. I talked about it on the phone with Gladys for hours on end.

Now I felt that I also had license to take my pains seriously, and in fact they began to get much worse. There was pain in my hip, pelvic bone, and leg, and I was having twinges in my lower back as well. I found it interesting that Gladys, with more than twenty metastatic lesions in her bones, suffered the most in the same places that were so painful for me.

In addition to a constant ache, I felt spasms whenever I put weight on my leg, and there were also spontaneous waves of pain that went through my whole body, accompanied by nausea. Sometimes I would go days without eating. Whenever I thought it couldn't get any worse, it did.

Painkillers weren't the answer. I had tried them. If they were mild, they didn't have any effect. If they were strong enough to shut out my pain, they put me in such a fog that I couldn't function or even knocked me out cold. And the pain always came back, calling my attention to it all over again. While of course it was logical to assume that it would return, relief always lured me into believing that my problem had been solved. It revived my optimism. When the pain did come back, I was always overwhelmed by a sinking, hopeless feeling.

Fortunately, work at the office demanded a fair amount of my attention. As irony would have it, the metastasis issue coincided with my return to a full-day schedule. The administrators had refused to extend my half-time arrangement any longer. Now I had more duties to perform and more responsibilities to worry about, and I was actually translating again, as well as experimenting with our own fledging machine translation system.

In my spare time, I was finishing up the project that Sylvio and I had started four years earlier. I thought it would never end. It had been a millstone around my neck, and for a while I felt as if I was working away at it with a nail file, but I finally began to see the end on the horizon. One bright note was that on my lunch hours I could key in the manuscript using the new word processing system at work. I thought word processing was the greatest invention since movable type and kept wishing that Sylvio could have lived to enjoy its advantages.

My mood picked up when a nice opportunity came along in mid-October. I was actually sent to La Jolla, California, on business. The trip gave me a vacation from my worries.

The bosses in the organization decided to send my colleague Marge and me to look into leasing an English-to-Spanish machine translation system from a company called SYSTRAN in La Jolla. I had known the developer of the software, Dr. Peter Toma, since my days as an undergraduate at Georgetown. In fact, he was a very dear friend. We had had many good times together, and he had a way of making me laugh. Sometimes we laughed so hard we couldn't stop and tears would come to our eyes. He had been extremely kind to me after my electroshock treatments many years earlier, and I am forever grateful to him for that—in fact, his kindness is one of the few good things I remember from that time of my life. For years he sent me flowers on my birthday. He knew that I loved lilacs in spring and shades of purple. We had each gotten married, and I had lost touch with him, but the friendship was still there, and I was really happy to see him when we got off the plane in San Diego.

The reunion was clouded by bad news when we arrived at the hotel. There was a message to call my mother. It turned out that my house back in Washington had been broken into and many things had been stolen, including all the jewelry and most of the silver serving pieces that Sylvio had given me. A neighbor actually witnessed the break-in and called the police. The siren scared off the burglars, and they dropped the stereo system as they ran away. The neighbor also called my mother, and Mother contacted a friend who came and boarded up the broken window. All this had happened while I was crossing the country in a plane. At first it felt like one more kick in the stomach. I didn't see how I would have the inner reserves to deal with yet another calamity. But those feelings melted in the warmth of my experience in La Jolla.

Peter and his staff made us feel very welcome. During our ten-day visit, their hospitality was so gracious that I managed to forget my recent loss and everything else that had been on my mind. My pains, though they weren't any better, were no longer my focus of attention. To my own surprise, I had a wonderful time. Marge and I worked hard studying the details of the Systran software and meeting with the staff, but when we weren't working we got to see many of the beauties and delights of Southern California. One day Peter drove up the coast on the old highway, stopping at one beach town after another, all the way to San Clemente.

On that trip, I was deeply moved by the meditation garden in Encinitas, perched on a cliff overlooking the ocean. The garden, which belongs to the Self-Realization Fellowship, features stone paths winding through lush tropical foliage, koi ponds connected by mini waterfalls, tree-shaded nooks, and benches both in secluded spots and out in the open for enjoying the ocean view. No words or pictures could possibly capture its full beauty. I was sure it was Heaven. I made up my mind at that moment that I wanted to live—or at least die—near this place that made me feel so serene and peaceful.

Afterwards, I kept having dreams about the garden and the ocean beyond. I felt a strong force pulling me there.

Back in Washington, I turned my attention to the insurance claim. The pieces that were stolen had been Sylvio's investment in my future, and the total value came to tens of thousands of dollars. Each estimate that I obtained felt like a new wound.

But my life had changed in a small, subtle way. Though I was still rehashing the same old thoughts and dealing unsuccessfully with my pains and nausea, I wasn't quite as worried as I had been before. California was in the back of my mind. La Jolla had opened me up. As with my trip to Norway, I was feeling cracks in the rigid thinking and the emotional wall I had built around myself.

Peter was calling me every night in an effort to lift my spirits and sending me large supplies of crystallized vitamin C. He encouraged me to take it in megadoses, and I got up to 25 grams a day, or 333 times the recommended daily allowance. At his insistence, I kept up the regimen for a long time. I'll never know if Peter's treatment made a significant difference, but in some ways I began to feel better.

My pain, however, kept getting worse.

Dr. Purcell put me in the hospital in mid-November, and I remained there for two weeks, taking one test after another. One of my least favorites was the spinal tap, which I considered nothing short of legalized torture. They also tried traction, which only intensified the pain, and physical therapy. The physical therapist told me that I wasn't "lax." She meant that I was pretty tensed up. This was actually the first time anyone had suggested that being more relaxed might help my situation. She tried heat and electrical muscle stimulation pads, to no effect. Nothing improved.

With the CT scan, my death wish almost came true. When iodine contrast was injected in my liver, I went into anaphylactic shock. I was unconscious for a long time and I'm told that my blood pressure dropped to 60/40. The hospital bed was tipped at a steep angle with my head down and my feet up, and doctors hovered over me all night.

I kept my sanity and shut out all that was going on around me by thinking and dreaming about the meditation garden in Encinitas.

Just before I left the hospital, Dr. Laird removed a "herniated lipoma" next to the lesion on my spine. It was a fatty tumor similar to what Sylvio had, but with a "twist." The idea was that removing it might relieve some pressure—not that it was the cause of my problem. The procedure was done under local anesthesia, and Dr. Laird kept me informed of progress:

"I see that we have a lipoma here. At least we're not going to come away empty-handed."

Afterwards, the pain in my back was better, but the situation in my hip and leg was unchanged. Dr. Laird said he also found a suspicious spot on the inside crest of my pelvic bone and tried to get Dr. Purcell to agree to biopsies of both the pelvis and the vertebra. He believed, as a matter of principle, that the only certain diagnosis is the one that can be seen under a microscope. But Dr. Purcell was still not ready to take that step.

The only concrete result that emerged from the two weeks of tests was that my CEA was still high. In other words, the indicators that led Dr. Laird and the oncologist at the clinic to believe I had metastasis were still there. Some other possible explanations for my pain had been ruled out, but nothing had really changed.

Dr. Purcell may not have found the evidence he needed to treat metastases in my bones, but I was still convinced that I had cancer.

When I went back to work, the medical referee was asking for a diagnosis and a report on my hospitalization. I called Dr. Purcell and told him about the request. He said he would write a report that said "absolutely nothing," and if they asked for more, I should tell them to "stick it in their ear."

I came home from the hospital just in time to start getting ready for Christmas. It was my first Christmas at home without Sylvio. I missed him as much as ever, and I was having mixed feelings about the holidays. There was a long list of cards to send and presents to buy and wrap, and I felt swamped and pressured—too much to do, and not enough time to do it in. It reminded me that Sylvio had always wanted Christmas to be simple. During my years with him, as soon as I opened the first box of decorations, he would start to say "Less is more"[31] in several different languages. What he wanted was for us to just spend time together. He thought that holiday preparations in the United States had come to completely overshadow the meaning of people being together; the means had become the end, and what it was really about had gotten lost. Back then, I didn't entirely agree with him.

There was one part of Christmas preparations that I really loved, and that was decorating the tree. It was my annual opportunity to bring out my inner artist. I had been collecting ornaments every year since I was twelve, and most of them had been hidden away in boxes for more than a decade. I had also bought some lovely new ones in Norway the year before, and festoons of little paper Norwegian flags. This year was my chance to have a tree once again, and I thought it might be my last. I decided to go all out. Friends helped me buy a big Scotch pine and put it up, and I covered it with hundreds of ornaments from countries all over the world. Those who saw it said they had never seen a prettier one.

In the bottom of one of the storage boxes I found a piece of folded newspaper on which Sylvio had written with a heavy marker pen: "The gift is small but the love is big." It was the wrapping he had used the year he gave me a diamond wedding band to replace the plain gold one I already had. The newspaper was symbolic of his disdain for fancy preparations. It brought tears to my eyes, and later I included it in a collage, along with other mementos of our Christmases together.

Today I fully share Sylvio's understanding of Christmas. The ornaments are back in their boxes, save for enough to cover a small tabletop tree. I get together with friends. Only a few inexpensive gifts are exchanged, stuffed along with tissue paper in handy pre-decorated bags. My messages to those I'm not able to see, more sincere than ever, are sent by e-mail and posted on Facebook. It took me a long time to see his point.

Mother and Aunt Muriel came in from the country to celebrate Christmas at my house, since it was difficult for me to drive. They arrived around noon on Christmas day. Mother brought a turkey she had cooked and all the trimmings. Sunshine couldn't get enough of the delicious smells. My main present for Mother was that I had managed, with great difficulty, to repair a delicate mobile of colorful birds that she was fond of. For some reason, she refused to accept it, and I felt hurt. Looking back, I wonder if she thought I should have it because she knew I liked it too, but at the time I understood that my effort had been rejected. On the other hand, I gave Aunt Muriel a subscription to *Mother Jones,* and she was thrilled. For once I did something right.

The atmosphere got tense when Aunt Muriel demanded to know when I was going to start treatment. I learned later that the two of them had been telling friends I was being treated with interferon. It was a total fabrication. Apparently they couldn't face the fact that nothing was happening. My answer was rude, and we all fell silent. As usual, Mother tried to patch things up between us, which meant that I was expected to apologize. I did, but the rest of the afternoon was awkward. That was our family dynamic in a nutshell.

When I was one on one with Mother, we were close and got along well, but my aunt had a strong influence over her.

Whenever Aunt Muriel was in the picture, pleasing her was my mother's top priority and she became a different person. My aunt's priority, at least the way I saw it, was putting me in my place. I always believed that she resented me more than she loved me. Our relationship had been fraught with tension from the beginning. Whatever the motivations behind their behavior, I felt unloved and abandoned on both sides. I would pout, overreact, or strain to control my feelings.

A few days after Christmas I saw Dr. Bittelmann, and I told him about my outburst and my other frustrations with Mother and Aunt Muriel. He pointed out that I was trying to read their signals and respond to them the way a child does. It was time for me to define myself in my own terms. I thought it was good advice, and I made a New Year's resolution to start working toward this goal. I recognized that working out my relationship with them was unfinished business.

17

I COULDN'T HELP BUT NOTICE THAT 1981 was an odd-numbered year. I was beginning to agree with Sylvio that the odd years were ill-fated. His forebodings about 1979 had been justified, and I noted that it was now four years since my partial mastectomy in January 1977. My outlook was gloomy. The weather was bitter cold and the ground was covered with snow and ice. On the phone, Peter told me it was 90 degrees in San Diego, which only made me even more upset with conditions in Washington.

It seemed as if everything was going wrong. My car kept breaking down, leaving me stranded in traffic several times, and I went through three batteries before someone figured out how to fix it. Machines at home were refusing to work. To top things off, big Norway rats had come up through the sewer and were lurking in the kitchen. Sometimes I saw them, and in the mornings I would find unpleasant signs of their presence the night before. Once a bed sheet had been stolen from the laundry pile, dragged across the dining room, and pulled through a 20-inch hole that had been chewed in the base of a built-in cabinet. The exterminator had tried the best he could, but in the end I had to have a valve installed in the sewer line, which was a costly, messy, and drawn-out process.

My pain was getting even more intense. The whole right side of my body was affected. My leg would buckle under me, causing me to fall. Sometimes I blacked out and collapsed. I got so I couldn't walk more than a few steps without having to stop and take the pressure off my leg. I carried a lightweight contraption that was both a cane and a stool so that I could sit down every few steps. It could take me an hour to get across a parking lot. Some days I couldn't walk at all. If portable walkers existed in the early 1980s, I wasn't aware of them. Even if they had been an option, I'm not sure I would have wanted to use one. I was resistant to admitting I had a problem, much less advertising it to the world.

In fact, it was difficult for me to admit that my pain was an ongoing challenge. I wasn't supposed to have it. Or was I? I have sometimes wondered if at some level I needed to punish myself. That may have been part of the story, but it would be an oversimplification. I was also very intent on denying that the pain existed at all. I was fighting its very existence, and the fight was making it worse.

Still, whether I wanted to or not, I had to make more and more arrangements just to keep going. My colleague Marge generously took over the job of getting me to and from the office. At home, one day my leg gave out and I tumbled all the way down the stairs, and after that, I took to sleeping in the living room. A neighbor walked Sunshine, and I had my cleaning lady get my groceries once a week. I started to make plans to move to a one-story apartment across the street. The future was frightening. I worried about becoming fully disabled and all that it would entail. I was angry at my body, and I wanted to get out of it.

On the other hand, I also began to wonder if my body was making a decision of its own. As I continued to grieve for Sylvio, I recalled the stories of couples who died within a short time of one another "of a broken heart." I read an article confirming that these events were not uncommon. It went on to say that the cause was stress—i.e., the stress caused by grieving, which sets the biochemical stage for illness. I wondered if something similar could be happening with me—if my natural defenses were shutting down from all the stress and struggle I was going through.

In mid-January, a Brazilian oncologist for whom I had done some work in the past arrived in Washington on an assignment. I showed him some of my medical records. After he had reviewed the papers, he said:

"Your patience is pathological. No normal human being would tolerate what you have been through."

I felt supported.

He, too, was in favor of a biopsy of my spine. He also had some other suggestions, and I gave him permission to speak with Dr. Purcell.

Perhaps as a result of their conversation, Dr. Purcell started me on the hormone drug tamoxifen. It was a big deal back then because it was new, though today it is widely used, even as a preventive. He couldn't understand the logic of my pain, but he did acknowledge that it existed, and he suggested that it was time to consider painkillers. Desperate, I let him give me a prescription and I had it filled. The pills did make me feel a little better—as long as the effect lasted

He sent me to an orthopedic surgeon, who was also reluctant to biopsy the bone. He confirmed that the lesion was in a delicate spot. As for the pain in my hip, he diagnosed it as severe tendonitis and likened it to "tennis elbow." Every time I took a step, I was re-injuring the tendon and it was getting more inflamed and scarred, which was adding to the pain that already existed. While the damage could be scraped off surgically, he said, "like barnacles on the bottom of a boat," it was not a permanent solution because the simple act of walking could re-create the same condition. He was optimistic that the process could be reversed without surgery. It would take a lot of patience and time—maybe months, or even years, he said. The idea was to rest the muscle and relax it so that it could gradually release the buildup of tension and allow the body to heal itself. As a first step, he started to give me cortisone injections in the hip. They gave me relief, but only for a few days. Even so, I began to understand that my leg would only get better if it was more relaxed.

I told Dr. Bittelmann what the orthopedist had said and asked if he thought it would make sense to take Valium to relax my muscles. He gave me a prescription for that, too.

For the first time, I was taking pills regularly, and for the first time I was having some respite now and then.

Despite these incremental steps forward, I went through a bad patch in mid-February, with pain so fierce that I could barely put my foot on the ground. One evening just before bedtime, the pain suddenly got much worse. The bottle of painkillers was empty, and I went crazy. I felt as if I couldn't go on one more minute. I had thought about being dead long enough, and I decided to make it happen. I sat down and started to write suicide notes. The messages didn't come easily to me. I wanted to write something meaningful, and I realized that I didn't have anything meaningful to say. I crumpled up a couple of drafts and finally settled on some wording that was less than ideal. I wrote three notes in all, and I put each one in an envelope.

Then I got out a razor blade, drew a bath, and got in. I looked at the razor, then looked at my wrists, then positioned the razor and got ready to cut. Just as I was about to do it, I stopped. I had been thinking of the notes, and I decided I could do better. If I was going to kill myself, my suicide notes had to be worthy. So I got out of the tub, dried myself off, and went back to re-write them. Even then I wasn't satisfied. Eventually I got tired of trying to say the right thing, and I gave up.

By that time the mood had passed and I decided not to go through with it. To make sure I wouldn't try it again, I thought of driving myself to an emergency room, but then I figured it would go on my record and lead to problems. As I look back, it's clear to me now that my desire to die wasn't as strong as I had thought it was—or else my will to live was stronger than I realized.

The crisis was over, but I was still desperate to relieve the pain. I went through all my drawers and closets until I finally found a stash of potent pills for menstrual cramps, smuggled from one of my trips to Latin America, and I gobbled down all that were left. I'm not sure if this was a desperate bid to stop the pain, another attempt to kill myself, or a little of both. The pills caused me to vomit, but they also did me the favor of knocking me out for the rest of the night.

I was all right the next morning. I stayed home reading, and just as the Universe sends us what we need to hear at the right time, I happened on the following line from Alexander King:

"Never underestimate the propulsive powers of despair—it can lead straight to glory, and sometimes even to a quiet heart."

I smiled to myself and felt a nudge of inspiration. The idea of a quiet heart appealed to me. After all the tumult, I realized that that was what I really wanted.

Part V

Turning Point

18

*In the depth of winter
I finally learned
there was inside me
an invincible summer.*
—Albert Camus

M Y FRIEND MARJORY CAME THROUGH town on her way from Mexico to Boston. I don't know if she detected a spark of hope in me, or if she wanted to give me encouragement, but once she arrived in Boston, she sent me a card with the verse above on the cover. I was very touched, and I framed the card and hung it on the wall next to my bed. Through all my moves since then, it has remained in that place of honor—a reminder of the changes that were about to happen.

My turning point came when I literally *heard* the effect of my own stressful thoughts attacking my body. I was sitting hooked up to biofeedback machines in a training lab when I was told to think a stressful thought. With my body perfectly still, my thought triggered a roar of electric static through the headphones—the sound of my inner works in a state of frenzy. This dramatic evidence of the power of a stressful thought started me on my path to healing.

Biofeedback uses machines[32] to tell us about activity inside our bodies that we are ordinarily not aware of. These are the same machines that are used in lie detectors. As wise as we may think we are, there is a secret world inside us that we are rarely in touch with. The biofeedback machines give us glimpses into that world. What we do with this "in-sight" is up to us.

I didn't know any of this when I enrolled in the biofeedback training in early March. Dr. Bittelmann had referred me for treatment. I had no idea what I was getting into, and I was leery of wasting any more time with experiments that didn't go straight to what I still believed was at the root of my problems—a galloping case of cancer that was being ignored, just like my nine-month wait back in 1976.

A week before the training was to start, I received a packet of materials in the mail, including a reading list and a bibliography. I still had a bad attitude about the whole thing and didn't do the assigned reading. However, I glanced at the bibliography and was impressed by the long list of scientific articles on biofeedback. I had had no idea that it was a serious field of study and the subject of so much research.

As events unfolded, I gradually came to understand that I was lucky to be part of an innovative program for managing stress, tension, and physical disease. I had been given the opportunity of a lifetime.

I remember the first day, and how difficult it was to walk from my car to the building. I was almost late because the pain in my hip was intense. It was one of those days when I had to rest after each step.

The training began with an orientation session for the group of us who were the Class of March 1981. We were all sick, and we had all been referred by our doctors. What I was about to learn became the foundation for my beliefs about health and disease.

The speaker explained vividly what happens to the body when stress is perceived, how this relates to illness, and what needs to be done to make the body whole again. He had my attention.

While I had heard about the "fight-or-flight" response, I had no idea how it related to disease. First I needed to understand what the body does to prepare itself for emergencies, and then, most important, what happens when it doesn't have a chance to return to normal.

I learned that we have one set of nerves to mobilize the body and another set to calm it down. The speaker drew pictures on the blackboard. The former are thin and wiry; they have little protection so they can transmit signals rapidly through cross talk. The latter, on the other hand, are heavily sheathed to reduce cross talk, and therefore they respond slowly and need time to do their job. *Our* job, as biofeedback trainees, was to understand this process and learn how to moderate it.

The body doesn't know the difference between real and imagined dangers. It "hears" everything that we think and feel, and it always goes through the same drill. While cave man had the chance to rest up between threats to his safety, today we are constantly bombarding ourselves with stressful thoughts and feelings. The effects accumulate, and we rarely get back to baseline.

The link to disease was becoming clear to me, and I was so excited that I could hardly sit still. It turns out that pain and disease are the worst stressors of all. They send constant stressful messages to the body. It can't heal when its signals are crossed. It has to get back to normal—or *homeostasis*.

That night I couldn't sleep; I kept thinking about what I had learned. Everything came together in my mind. I could see how stress adds to illness and makes healing impossible – a scenario that had been totally alien to me only a week earlier.

My training program was to be eight weeks of individualized sessions plus follow-up. At my first one-on-one session with the therapist, the focus was on teaching me to relax. I thought to myself: How insulting is *that*? Of course I know how to relax! But I could not have been more wrong. I had volumes to learn about the simple process of letting go.

She attached me to four of the machines—but not the headphones—and told me to relax. At this point the feedback was for *her* benefit, not mine. She gave me an arithmetic task to work in my head and said:

"Keep going until I tell you to stop. The answer you give at that point will be compared with other responses of people in your age group.

I calculated feverishly for several long minutes. When the time was up and I gave her my answer, I asked her how I did. She confessed that she wasn't interested in my answer; she had been watching the readings on the machines. I felt that she had tricked me, but of course her whole purpose was to make me feel stressed. She monitored me once again, to see how readily I got back to a relaxed state. The figures she collected would be the baseline for measuring my future progress.

There was homework—two kinds. For the next five weeks, every hour on the hour (even through the night whenever I was awake), I was to check my body for any tenseness and rate how strongly I felt it on a scale from 0 to 5, then do the same thing for pain. The two sets of ratings were plotted on a graph to form curves. It didn't take long to see a clear relationship between tension and my pain. The feedback was visual.

There was also a set of tapes. They introduced progressive relaxation and included a lot of visualizations. Each time I played a tape, I was to evaluate how deeply I had relaxed on a scale from 0 to 10 and make notes about all the sensations I experienced. I could see that my pain was getting better all the time. The tapes became a habit, and sometimes I practiced with them for more than two hours a day.

In the meantime, the orthopedist prescribed a TENS[33] machine, which I was supposed to wear attached to my hip at all times. I got it working, and its little staccato became an accompaniment to the tapes. My friend Marge jokingly warned me not to get a "short circuit" while doing both at the same time. For a while, it was the meter of my existence. It helped me a little, but not a lot.

Over the next seven weeks I continued to do my homework and check in at the center once a week for counseling and monitoring on the machines. Every day brought a new revelation, but my progress was uneven. I will leave it to some of the entries in my diary to tell how the experience unfolded.

Friday, March 6. "I can't do the tape with my glasses off. I feel too vulnerable without them."

Saturday, March 7. "The tape is getting to me! This morning I woke up really angry at it and couldn't bring myself to play it. All day long my Bad Angel was saying that I *enjoy* being tense. When the voice on the tape says "Notice that tight, cramped, unpleasant feeling,' I keep wanting to say 'But I *like* it!'"

Sunday, March 8. "Now I see what was happening. I was afraid that not being tense meant *losing control*. Wow! Once I understood this, things began to fall into place. I was able to take off my glasses! As it turned out, I had good reason to worry: I realized that I *am* vulnerable. For some reason, recognizing this has set me free. Now I can say 'So what?!'"

Monday, March 9. "Tonight the TENS was on. To my surprise, I fell into a deeply relaxed state. I was floating, and I felt tingly and 'mentholated' when the muscles let go."

Tuesday, March 10. "Today was my second session with the therapist. My readings for muscle tension were dramatically improved. I impressed her with my observation about losing control. She asked me what had 'tipped me off,' and I told her about the glasses.

"I got to use the headphones for the first time! The *real* biofeedback. The noise was a gentle clicking sound that began to race and get louder when my muscles tensed up, turning into a storm. First I listened with my fists clenched as tightly as possible; then I relaxed and got the clicks down to almost zero, just few and far between.

"Then the therapist told me to stay completely relaxed and think of something stressful. I thought about my diagnosis. To my amazement, the sound came rushing back just as loud and fast as when I had clenched my fists, even though I was certain that my body was totally relaxed. *There was no difference!!"*

It was almost too much to believe that my thoughts had exactly the same effect on my body as when I tightened my muscles as hard as I could. That moment was my epiphany. I became aware, at my deepest level, that my thoughts drive the unconscious processes going on in my body. I understood that I had a choice: I could choose to harbor stressful thoughts, or I could release my attachment to them before they launched on a destructive path—on that poisonous journey that only harms myself. The opportunities were infinite.

19

IT SEEMS LIKE YESTERDAY WHEN I heard that storm in my ears, triggered only by a stressful thought. However, as important as that moment was, my training had just begun and many more lessons awaited me. There was a lot of homework, and I was a slow learner. I kept on practicing my relaxation tapes, but with a new appreciation of my purpose.

My diary continued.

Thursday, March 12. "It's becoming automatic: when I begin to feel that tension is building up, my response is to relax. It takes the place of so many other, less healthy responses I could have if I feel stressed. It's something I can do 200 or 1,000 times a day, not only with impunity but with the satisfaction that something good is happening."

Friday, March 13. "My lower jaw is beginning to relax. I see that jaw-clenching is linked to the muscle in my forehead. My therapist called it the *frontalis* and told me it's the first muscle that babies learn to contract. It reflects tension all over the body. That's why they put the electrodes there.

"I like differential relaxation. It's about tensing up some parts while relaxing the rest. I can practice it anywhere. It helps me with my lame hip. At first I couldn't keep it tense for very long, but I got better with practice, and afterward I could finally let go. I've noticed that the pain has improved a great deal this week."

Monday, March 16. "The new tape says 'My arms are heavy and warm,' but they're *not*. They're light and cool. I want to go up, to levitate. It scares me to be heavy and sink down."

Thursday, March 19. "Sometimes my mind wanders with the tape, and I've been fighting this tendency, feeling that I'm doing the exercise wrong and, worse still, wasting my time. I try to visualize a lake and imagine my thoughts being carried across it on a breeze. Let them come; the wind will move them along. Now I realize it's important not to try to block them; if I accept them and don't fight them, they move on more easily."

Friday, March 20. "During the tape this morning I drifted off on a cloud and was overtaken by delicious shudders of pleasure. I was warm all over. Then afterwards, for the first time, the feeling carried over into the rest of my day and I was pleasantly relaxed."

Sunday, March 22. "I keep getting wiser. I hadn't realized how important it is to relax the muscles in my *neck*. My cervical pillow came in the mail. When I lie down, it separates my head and my body like a watershed. Both parts let go. On one side, all the muscles relax in my head and jaw; on the other, I feel the tingles run down my spine as each vertebra lets go, one after the other.

"I'm guessing that the jaw carries so much tension because it's reading from our mind all the impulses we have to say things. As if it's talking our thoughts. It's constantly at the ready, preparing to formulate those millions of messages that never get expressed."

Monday, March 23. "My therapist helped me realize that much of the pressure in my office is self-imposed.

"About the pain, it's still there but I'm managing it better, and now I try not to respond to it by tensing up. Also, I don't let it upset me, and I've stopped worrying about what it means."

Thursday, March 26. "Dr. Bittelmann reminded me not to get worked up about my scores on the machines. He pointed out that in the history of biofeedback no one had ever *flunked*. I try not to be concerned; my life is working ever so much better, and that's all that counts."

Sunday, March 29. "I'm meeting situations more calmly, driving the car more carefully, and working smoothly, efficiently, and with more energy. Nothing is more important, or more pleasurable, than the rich sensations that are coming into my life.

"Everyone is commenting on my new appearance. These changes are helping to improve my outlook and make me feel more encouraged about the future. Sylvio had always wanted me to learn to relax. I wish he could be here now!"

Monday, March 30. "At my session today I told my therapist about all the shifts that have been taking place. She noted that the effects of stress accumulate in the body over years. I told her I thought it would be great if children could learn about it in school, as prevention rather than therapy for damage already done. She was pleased with my enthusiasm.

"'We like zealots,' she said.

"My pain is definitely not as bad. For the first time in months, last week I was able to work 40 hours in the office. There are longer periods of relative relief. I attribute this to better management, less tension, and a more accepting outlook. The idea of being stuck with pain doesn't upset me any more."

Tuesday, March 31. "I can really see that relaxation frees up my powers of concentration. In order to *see* things, I have to be *open* to them.

"I also see that awareness of tension is a mixed blessing. While it alerts me to the need to relax, it also makes me painfully conscious of discomfort in my body that I was never aware of before. Now, if someone interrupts me, it feels like an invasion. The pain comes back in my hip. And I feel frustrated because I can't control what other people do."

Saturday, April 4. "I'm working on the muscles in my face. Part of the tension comes from the jaw and part from the tongue. I'm so aware of my tongue that my mouth hurts. My therapist said that the tongue is the last muscle in the body to relax, so maybe I'm on the home stretch."

Wednesday, April 8. "I've been off my feed(back)—literally. All afternoon I was hounded by tension in my jaw, and nothing I did seemed to make it any better. I called up my therapist and asked her if I could borrow the portable jaw monitor they lend out and try it at home when I'm sleeping."

Friday, April 10. "I picked up the jaw device yesterday. Tried it out last night. At first it kept me awake beeping every time I clenched my jaw, but after a while I got the hang of it and was able to relax so it wouldn't beep. I can keep it for two weeks."

Monday, April 13. "We talked about cancer being a process, a disruption in an ecosystem, rather than simply a lump."

Tuesday, April 14. "Today has been one of those perfect days that make winter seem like it never happened. I'm delighted to announce that my improvement has kept pace with the change in season. The pain is much better. I am bubbling with energy. I feel great! I should have known: the 'invincible summer' was there inside me!"

My journal ends here. I had started it to document the progress of my disease—decades before stories of the kind were shared on the Internet—and at this point I realized that I was defeating my own purpose.

Thanks to biofeedback, I now fully grasped the mechanism of stressful thoughts and understood the damage that they do. I had been deceiving myself when I believed that thinking and writing about cancer would make me better. Instead, I was beating up my body and making it sicker. My obsession with the details was undermining my health and actually aggravating the problem that I thought I was solving.

Also, I was soon to discover that I hadn't been fully invested in getting well. At the very least, I was holding onto cancer because it was a welcome distraction, sparing me from emotional pain that I still couldn't bear to feel and crowding out what I didn't want to face—including fear itself. Paradoxically, poring over the details kept me from looking at fear and other challenging emotions that I needed to acknowledge and understand before I could deal with them.

20

M<small>Y BIOFEEDBACK THERAPIST TOLD ME</small> that the Simontons were coming to town and recommended that I attend their one-day event at Maryland University. She explained that the Simontons were a married couple who had been using biofeedback to treat cancer with impressive results. The program sounded interesting, and I decided to sign up. When I called to register, the first thing the woman said was:

"Do you have cancer?"

I told her that I did.

Her next question stunned me. Her voice was gentle, but clear and firm:

"Are you prepared to assume responsibility for your disease?"

I didn't know what to say. After a long pause, while I was trying to figure out what she meant, she stepped into the silence and explained that participants who had cancer were expected to ask themselves this question and think seriously about the answer. I swallowed and took the plunge:

"Yes, I'm prepared to take responsibility."

The idea was alien to me, but I started to process it, remembering all that I had recently learned from biofeedback.

While I knew a lot about stress and certainly recognized its role in disease, what I hadn't understood was that I, personally, bore responsibility. The woman's question brought it home to *me*. My answer was an important and necessary step in the process of getting well. Taking that step was worth the price of admission.

The Simontons arrived on a sunny day in April. The large auditorium was packed with several hundred people. Carl Simonton, a radiation oncologist, led the morning's program on the role of emotions in cancer. In the afternoon, his wife Stephanie, a psychologist, talked about using imagery in treating cancer, and a former patient, Robert Gilley, spoke on "Learning to Live Without Cancer." I did a double-take on the last title. I had always thought that the challenge was to live *with* cancer. For the first time I realized that there was an art to living *without* cancer.

The husband-and-wife team had recently published their book, *Getting Well Again: A Step-by-Step Self-Help Guide to Overcoming Cancer for Patients and Their Families*.[34] I had time to buy a copy before the workshop started, and I also bought a book titled *Stress, Psychological Factors, and Cancer*,[35] which summarized the scientific research that had been done on the role of stress in cancer.

With my purchases in hand, I settled into a seat about halfway back in the auditorium. As people in the audience later identified themselves, it became apparent that about half of them were cancer patients and most of the rest were health care professionals. The woman on my right was clutching a folder labeled "pain management." I hadn't thought that pain was something that could be "managed," and the phrase piqued my curiosity.

Carl's talk was about guilt, fear, helplessness, and hopelessness.

I had a long history with guilt, so I listened closely. He emphasized that guilt doesn't have energy. For this reason, it doesn't move us anywhere. Nothing gets accomplished if we use it to solve the problems it has created. Because it feeds on itself, it boxes us in. Suddenly I was able to put the pieces together: my guilt was a misguided attempt to punish myself for perceived wrongdoings, and I was doomed to keep punishing myself because it was a feedback loop from which I could never escape. I would always be trying, and my efforts would never be enough. I thought about the decades I had spent holding onto my guilty memories: first my grandfather, then my baby, and then Sylvio, and the underlying self-talk in which I took on guilt about almost everything else as well. My guilt had turned me into a lifelong prisoner. My attempt to make up for my transgressions was not only ineffective and a waste of time, it was also destructive: I was poisoning myself. Once I understood what was happening, I saw my path to freedom: since I was already learning how to deal with thoughts that were "stressful," I could try to do the same with thoughts about guilt. They were no different, just deeper.

Carl continued. Fear, unlike guilt, has energy. That makes it easier to deal with. He proposed that one way of coping with a particular fear is to move directly into it—conjure up a fantasy of it in its fullest, wildest possible form. When carried to the extreme, it gets to be preposterous. To illustrate, he described a creepy-crawly vision of what cancer might look like if we could see it. He managed to make it sound funny, and everyone laughed, including me. For a moment at least, fear about cancer seemed ridiculous.

If we allow fear to take hold, he said, it can lead to helplessness. When we are ill, we feel especially vulnerable. We tend to lean on others and let them figure out how to get us well. This is a state in which helplessness flourishes and expands.

If helplessness goes unchecked, he explained, it turns into hopelessness. He called this the "no exit place"—that point at which we become convinced there is nothing that can make us better. It is probably the most painful of all life experiences, he said. We naturally want to avoid it, because we know it's painful. So we deny it. He cautioned that there are times when it's appropriate to feel hopeless, and in fact it's crazy not to.

Dealing with hopelessness, he pointed out, is not as easy as dealing with fear. But recognizing it, rather than denying it, is the first step. We could start to tackle it by practicing responses to small daily frustrations that tend to make us feel helpless. As we approach a challenge, we can consider how to cut it down or divide it up—in other words, ask less of ourselves. That idea was very freeing for me. It became a strategy that I have tried to apply ever since. When faced with a challenge that seems like too much, I stop to analyze it and see if there are ways I can bring it down to size.

So how do we change? Carl offered some solutions. First of all, we must accept where we are. We should not deny or avoid it. Change in itself is stressful, and we can only set the stage to allow it to happen. He said:

"The process starts with: 'I need to change around that, and I don't know how' . . ."

Carl emphasized that we don't *need* to know how—any more than we needed to know how to be born. The key is to be able to slow down, relax, and be open to it. If we can do that, the solution will eventually come. "A personal program to slow down cannot be hurried up."

All that he said hit home for me. I had been tied up in guilt; I hadn't faced my fears; I had been feeling helpless and leaning on doctors to give me answers that were inside me; and, with the help of reports of metastasis, I had fallen into hopelessness. It was time to change, and the only way to do it was to relax and let it happen. Carl had taken me by surprise and opened up my world in ways I had never expected. Without my breakthrough with biofeedback, I would not have been ready for this next big step.

In the question-and-answer period that followed, a gentle, attractive young woman of about 30, Mary Catherine, went up to the microphone to ask for advice in dealing with her mother. Mary had had several surgeries for metastasized breast cancer and the outlook was not very hopeful. Her mother kept asking her if she was afraid, and she found it upsetting. She wanted Carl to tell her how to get her mother to leave her alone. His answer took the form of the following dialogue:

Carl: Now, pretend that you are your mother, and I will pretend that I'm you. Have her ask me a question. Go on . . .

Mary Catherine (pausing briefly to switch into her now role): Darling, aren't you *scared*?

Carl: **OF COURSE I'M SCARED!! D'YA THINK I'VE GOT SHIT FOR BRAINS?!?**

His voice boomed, and the auditorium shuddered with the shock of his metaphor. I shuddered, too, with the reality of my own fear. I felt it from my head to the soles of my feet. Tears kept welling up as I struggled to hold them back. I *was* afraid. It would be stupid not to be. Through all my soul-searching and journal-writing, I had sidestepped looking at fear. I had gone through a range of emotions, but I had never fully faced the big one.

But what was I afraid of? The first thing that came to mind, of course, was death itself. I was afraid of it because I don't know what's on the other side. The unknown is always scary. I had given a lot of thought to death, but I hadn't realized that the unknowable was the part I feared the most. Then I realized that I was afraid of *how* I was going to die. At first that was very scary, but I didn't really know why. I had to separate my thoughts from the churning going on inside me. Death from cancer could be painful, but I was used to pain. If I took away dying and pain, what else about cancer was I afraid of? I was afraid of being incapacitated and bedridden and alone in the world. It was harder to let go of that idea, because I thought of all that it entailed: giving up my home, not having a job, becoming nobody. In fact, being nobody was *very* frightening. Indeed, there were many valid reasons to be afraid. I tried to think of more.

Then I realized that underneath the specifics were horrors that were nameless, shapeless, unidentified, and unidentifiable— those monsters that lurk in the darkness of the construct "cancer" itself. Looking more closely, I saw that they were empty and meaningless. I had taken on fears that I couldn't even begin to describe. Some may have been products of my own psyche; others, an echo of society's beliefs.

Now that all this was out in the open, I saw that my fears could be dealt with. The more I started to take them apart and look at each one separately, the less formidable they turned out to be. But it was the vague and faceless chimeras with no substance that had been the biggest force behind my helplessness and hopelessness. I finally understood: my fears, just like the vulnerability I had discovered in biofeedback, had to be acknowledged and embraced, and only then could I begin to let go of them.

In the afternoon I was too excited to sit still and concentrate. I left the workshop early. I had had all I could process in a single day. My whole world had started to spin, and I felt sad, dizzy, exuberant, overwhelmed—and free. I spent the rest of the afternoon going over my notes from Carl's talk and sitting, thinking deeply, in the garden labyrinth of the church where Sylvio's funeral was held. The workshop had surely been another giant step on my journey.

That night I started reading Carl's book, *Getting Well Again*. The first sentence reinforced everything I had learned, and it reminded me that being well was a full-time undertaking:

"Everyone participates in his or her health or illness at all times."

At first it overwhelmed me to think that the body never stops listening. Every discouraging thought or feeling is registered, and it sets the stress process in motion, eventually creating disease if it continues uninterrupted. Then I realized that the body also responds to joy, laughter, and hope. Each moment is an opportunity to release old patterns, embrace new ideas, reinforce positive thoughts—and to laugh.

The book tells of many so-called "terminal" patients who followed the Simonton program and long outlived their predicted lifespan. And they did so living a life of quality and joy.

I understand now that the real trick is learning to *live* cancer-free, even in the face of treatment and tests that may indicate otherwise.

The Simontons encourage patients to ask themselves if they have any reasons why they might *not* want to be well again—what they call "secondary gains." Is something keeping them from wanting to solve their problems? Does illness have any payoffs for them? This is a tough question, and I considered what the payoffs might be for me. I believe that in my case thinking about illness gave focus to my otherwise sad and empty life. It distracted me from facing my deep feelings about grief and guilt. But I also

135

asked myself a few other questions: Was it a bid for sympathy? Did I want to be taken care of? Or was I ready to give up because life was just too hard without Sylvio? The answers weren't as important as the fact that I was even open to considering these questions.

The program has a simple four-point formula for getting well again. Patients must expect that they are going to recover. They have to be confident that they are in charge of their disease. They need a positive focus for their energy. And they have to have a healthy self-image, which includes acceptance of their cancer.

My attitude still needed work in two areas: I hadn't decided that I was going to recover, and I didn't have a focus for my energy. On the other hand, I had gained a sense that I was in charge of my disease, and I understood about accepting cancer. I knew that as long as we are fighting a battle inside, our chances of winning are diminished. We can't afford to hate our cancer because it means that we are hating ourselves. We do best by embracing those parts of ourselves that we don't like and ceasing to judge them. In this way, we break up harmful patterns and let go of them more easily.

It is now more than thirty years later, and unfortunately the Simonton message has not spread very far. While there have been huge strides in laboratory research and cancer treatment, the majority of cancer patients continue to send their body angry and depressing messages about their disease. Our culture still glorifies the "warriors" who "fight" cancer. Their "battle" is celebrated as if they were at war with an alien attacker. Treatments are routinely referred to as "weapons," "bullets," and "arsenal." War takes focus, and what we focus on expands. The real path for all of us is to embrace our fears, relax deeply, and love every part of our body, the perfect creation that it is—even, and most especially, if it has cancer.

21

I WAS SURE THAT MY FRIENDS were fed up hearing me talk about biofeedback, so I was surprised when three fellow translators signed up for a six-hour biofeedback workshop at a local college. It was late June 1981, and I had "graduated" from my training. They encouraged me to join them, to see how the workshop compared with what I had been taught at the center. Given the months I had invested attending training sessions and practicing the principles almost around the clock, I thought it was hardly possible that I could learn anything new in two three-hour sessions, but I agreed to go along. I quickly discovered that I still had a lot to learn. In fact, I was about to embark on a process that healed my pain once and for all and took everything I had learned to a new level.

Our instructor, Lorraine, was a pretty, petite bundle of energy with a bottomless bag of tricks. While the program at the center took itself very seriously, with Lorraine biofeedback was *fun*. My therapist had warned me more than once that it was a powerful prescription that shouldn't be fooled around with, and she even cautioned me against recommending it to my friends. Lorraine, on the other hand, wanted to share the good news with everyone. Her people were clients, not patients.

Everything in its season. I had learned the basics in boot camp, and now I was ready for the next level. I was soon to gain a whole new perspective on managing stress.

While the program at the center had emphasized the biology of stress and how it contributes to illness in general, Lorraine cited facts and mentioned specific diseases by name. I knew about the connection, of course, but the list of disease names drove the point home and started me thinking about other health challenges besides my own.

After warning us of its consequences, however, she quickly drew a distinction between stress itself and how we perceive it. When people talk about "stress," they are really referring to the *perception* of stress.

"Stress is not an enemy," she said. It has gotten a bum rap. It can be positive. We need it in our lives. It has an important place in making the world go around. Instead of fighting it off, we can change how it affects us. She added:

"Stress itself doesn't cause symptoms. It's our response to it that does."

At the center we had worked on changing our perception of *situations*, but Lorraine was talking about how we perceive stress itself. To her, stress is no more than a message telling us that we may want to program our lives differently. It is valuable information, showing us where to pay attention in organizing our lives.

Rather than starting with deep relaxation, Lorraine introduced some mental strategies for dealing with stress. Two of them would become part of my regular practice: visualization and a technique for changing the outcome of dreams. She also gave us some coping strategies—for example, time management and assertiveness techniques—to preempt situations that could bring up stressful feelings. I began to see stress in a different light. It was simply a fact of life, and I had the tools for handling it.

She explained that we eventually lose sensitivity in the muscles we tense up most often, especially in the forehead and the jaw. She had us imagine ourselves as puppets, hanging limply from strings, while our scalp was being massaged by tiny fingertips. Our necks became cooked spaghetti—she promised us that our heads wouldn't fall off. Our arms turned into molten wax; our eyelids, two soft blankets. Our buttocks settled into wet clay.

Then she introduced the machines—junior versions of the ones I was familiar with. She emphasized that *all* symptoms and *all* emotions, without exception, are registered as tension in the muscles. She explained that tension in the skeletal muscles is easier to control consciously than other physical responses to stress. Skin temperature tells us how long it takes for adrenaline to stop flowing: once our hands are warm, we can know that the body is back to its job of taking care of itself.

When she led us through relaxation, her phrases were imaginative and her voice was reassuring. She helped us feel that, no matter what happens when we relax, it's all good. Sudden twitching and jerking is a sign that we are on track to going even deeper. It's okay if our heads feel warm instead of cool. If we want to float instead of getting heavy and sinking down, that's perfect, too. Whatever we feel right with is the way we should feel.

In the second session Lorraine asked us to pay attention to a particular symptom and visualize something that would make it feel good. By that time the pain in my hip was a lot better, but it was still there. I imagined that it was a small bed of hot coals, and that as I relaxed, soft rain was falling on the coals, putting out the fire. The image worked quite well, and I felt better afterwards. I got the sense that if I repeated the exercise daily, my pain would gradually get better.

Lorraine's closing gift to us was the concept of *basking*. Whenever we become aware of something positive or beautiful in our lives, she would have us stop time and lock in the essence of the good feeling—not do anything else, just appreciate how good it feels. She emphasized that it's important to enjoy a positive sensation. All too often we go right back to our old worries.

The following week I started seeing Lorraine as a client in her private practice. It was the beginning of a thirteen-year relationship, until I left Washington.

Lorraine sees her clients in her home—to spare herself the stress of commuting. She creates a warm and comfortable environment with walls painted a shade of pink that is known to induce relaxation.

We started out by working on the visualization that I had developed in the workshop. I refined it and added some extra details: the rain that put out the coals turned into a soft, soothing ointment. I decided that the ointment had healing properties, like the white cells in a visualization exercise developed by the Simontons. I let it spread out and envelop the rest of my body.

While I was perfecting my visualization and getting it to work, Lorraine introduced me to a technique called Open Focus™.[36] Adapting it to my own case, she prepared two tapes for me.

To make the message personal, she addressed me by name:

"Muriel, begin this exercise by just closing your eyes and allowing yourself to get very, very comfortable . . ."

She reminded me on the tape that my body knows exactly what to do, that I am just allowing the process to happen. She told me to breathe deeply, gently . . . not "mightily" . . . and "feel the heartbeat in my fingertips . . ." The message went on from there, relaxing each part of the body. Then she had me imagine that all the nooks and crannies between the body parts were filled with empty space.

In the second tape, I was to visualize empty spaces next to and around the ones that I had already created. Gradually all the spaces merged together to form one great big openness with me inside it. Or *was* I? The boundaries of my body were gone. I was no longer aware of my own substance. More than that, there was a vastness to the experience that was a trillion times more powerful than anything I had felt before. I was at one with the Universe!

I practiced the tapes at home, and at our next session, once I had reached the "vastness," or Open Focus, Lorraine directed me to go back to the pain in my hip. I could feel the pain starting to break up! If it had made a noise, it would have crackled. Then slowly she sent me back to the vastness, and then once more to the hip. All of a sudden the whole pain jarred loose! Like a material being with a life of its own, it jumped from my right hip over to the left one, paused there for a few moments, and then traveled down my left leg and out through my toes. It was the first time

I had felt total release from the pain since it had started almost two years earlier. I was delirious with joy. As I walked out onto the street, bells were chiming everywhere. It felt as if the bells were for me, but it was July 29, 1981, and they were celebrating the royal newlyweds, Prince Charles and Diana.

The pain did come back, but it was no longer attached to hopelessness. The more I listened to Lorraine's tapes, the less intense it became.

My life was turning around in major ways, and I decided to stop seeing Dr. Bittelmann. He agreed that I was doing well and that it was time for me to "graduate."

Meanwhile, the great results I was having with Lorraine inspired me to send away for more materials from the developer of Open Focus, Lester Fehmi. The kit came with an article explaining how it works. It is a technique to help people stop trying so hard when they're practicing deep relaxation. I recognized myself right away, trying just as hard at relaxation as everything else, when "trying hard" was a big part of my problem in the first place. Fehmi had studied the brain waves of biofeedback trainees in his lab and noticed that they tended to rivet their focus on specific perceptions.

That certainly applied to me. For two years I had focused on a small set of thoughts having to do with Sylvio, pain, cancer, Sylvio, pain, cancer, Sylvio, pain . . . in a repeating loop.

Narrow focus, I learned, goes along with tension, repression, anxiety, and other difficult states. It is a major block to relaxation. As narrow perceptions break up, these attitudes fall away. Fehmi makes this happen by getting people to empty objects from the mind's eye.

It didn't take long for me to realize that Open Focus applies equally as well to emotional pain. I understood at a deeply experiential level that being in Open Focus is a way of life. After that, when I caught myself narrowing in on a thought, I would remember the tapes and that delicious moment when all body awareness disappears, I am floating euphorically among the stars, and the message on the tape says:

"Everything is equal. . ."

22

As I OPENED MYSELF UP, more new lessons continued to appear. I took Werner Erhard's est training[37] about a year after I started with Lorraine. I learned a lot, though not necessarily what the program set out to teach me.

I had never heard of est, and I let myself get roped into it. You could almost say I was shanghaied. In the late summer of 1982 my friend Mary Lou invited me to what I thought was going to be an evening of entertainment. It turned out to be a "guest seminar" for recruiting new est trainees. Shortly after we arrived, I was hustled into a room with a group of other potential recruits, where we were each assigned a "leader" to work us over, one on one. My leader was Jennifer.

Of course, Jennifer's job was to get me to sign up for the training and pay a chunk of money. She wasn't allowed to go into specifics, so her main talking points were:

It will blow your mind! It will transform you!

A new training was about to start. It was a 60-hour program—two full week-ends and two Wednesday evenings. The official purpose, I later learned, was "to transform one's ability to experience living so that the situations one had been trying to change or had been putting up with, clear up just in the process of life itself."[38]

I wasn't interested for several reasons. To begin with, I didn't have either the time or the money. Second, I was already going through a lot of transformation and wasn't sure I wanted to handle more, especially without knowing anything about the program, its goals, and so on. And finally, I had my back up because I felt I had been tricked into coming and was being pressured into signing up. I told Jennifer I couldn't do it. However, she was prepared with an answer to every objection I raised. When I said I had a term paper due at school and a grant proposal to write in the next two weeks, she laughed:

"But that's just the *point*! That's what the training is all about. After your training, you'll be able to get your work done in half the time!"

She was a writer herself, and she claimed that est had given her a phenomenal boost in productivity. I did feel swamped, and she got me where I was vulnerable. I began to waver. Before I realized it, I was writing a check for $475—a lot more than cold prudence would normally have allowed me to part with.

The training took place in the ballroom of a chain hotel deep in the Virginia suburbs. There were two hundred of us. All hues, creeds, and ages were represented, as well as vastly different mindsets, life experiences, and degrees of self-awareness. The est approach was aimed at everyone. One size fit all. The harshness that may have been effective for some was a turnoff for me. We were all "assholes," no exceptions. The first day was mainly devoted to weeding out the people who couldn't—at least temporarily—accept that they were assholes. The trainer hammered on each of them to try to talk them out of their beliefs. If they stood their ground, they were allowed to drop out and get their money back. I can't explain why I didn't leave. Perhaps I was too meek to walk out in the presence of the large roomful of people, or maybe I was priding myself on keeping an open mind. Certainly I was hoping that something better lay in store.

There were some presentations and processes, but most of the time was spent in dialogue with individual trainees. On Saturday night we were kept in stiff, uncomfortable chairs with few "bathroom breaks" until three o'clock in the morning. Sunday we left a couple of hours earlier, around one o'clock. Then there was an hour-long drive home. I was exhausted. My brain felt like cotton. I literally could not form a picture in my mind—it was a blank white space. I wondered if that was what it meant to be brain-washed.

By the end of the first day I had a better understanding of what the training was about. Most of the teachings made sense to me: not getting caught up in our own dramas, letting go of what doesn't serve us, avoiding negative thinking, being confident, standing up when we speak, not hiding behind "props," communicating clearly and concisely, being totally honest, keeping all commitments, finishing what we start, honoring the moment we are in over the past or the future, and others. It was all perfectly good advice, but I thought it was more of a hodge-podge than an integrated set of principles. My problem was with the rigid and extreme training methods.

I must not have been brain-washed, because I was still sticking to my own beliefs. The est rules made no exceptions, whereas I believe in grays, rather than all black or all white. I believe that an event is always shaped by multiple factors and causes. I believe in not judging people. I believe that, as a goal, we honor the commitments that we make, but there may also be times when the wiser choice is to let go. But I knew better than to speak up.

By the final Sunday morning I was ready to conclude that the experience had been largely a waste. However, I changed my mind when the trainer got into a lecture on "The Anatomy of the Mind." It was worth all the time and money I had invested. My long wait was rewarded. Using vivid, cartoon-like images, the trainer showed that when memories get stored in the mind, they can get hooked up to emotions that may be inappropriate or irrelevant to the context in which the events actually happened. New experiences get networked in with similar ones from the past, creating a cumulative effect. The point was that we have the choice to unhook the emotions that are attached to both our current experiences and our recollections. This explanation appealed to me.

I recalled the image of Sylvio in the hospital on the last day of his life, and for the first time I was able to separate the memory from the emotions around it. I could *detach* them. The scene, which up to then had been too horrifying to process, was suddenly neutralized. In the space of a split second I freed myself from the waking nightmare that had overpowered my existence for the last three years.

After this big breakthrough, everything else seemed dull and silly. I sat patiently for the rest of the day, though I wanted to get out in the world and celebrate. At eleven o'clock in the evening, just before a bathroom break, the remaining program was announced. I calculated (correctly, it turned out) that the seminar would be going on for at least another five hours. I had to be in the office early the next morning for an important meeting. I decided to do the unthinkable: I simply walked out. At the exit from the parking lot, two male estians tried to flag me down and stop me, but I kept on driving.

An hour later I was home and already in my nightgown when the doorbell rang. It was Mary Lou. As my sponsor, she had gone to the meeting to participate in my graduation, only to find that I wasn't there. I didn't let her in, so she stood there awkwardly on the doorstep, pleading for me to go back. The whole group was upset, she said. Everything had stopped, and they were waiting for me. I had betrayed them. But her main concern was that the "incomplete" would ruin me for the rest of my life.

She wouldn't give up. I finally told her that I would have to close the door. She offered me a deal: she would leave if I would let her use the phone. She came in and called the trainer back at the hotel. When he got on the line, she held the receiver to my ear. He talked *at* me for what seemed like half an hour, stating repeatedly that my life was all "fucked up" and that I would die of cancer if I didn't go back and learn to complete my incompletes. I don't know if he knew I'd had cancer, or if it was part of his script. I was unmoved. I had already made my decision not to have cancer. Now my decision was to stay home and get some sleep. No hard feelings. Mary Lou finally left.

I'm sorry if my fellow trainees were let down because I didn't respect the integrity of the group and stay with them to the end.

I hope it was just a passing feeling. I wish they could know how much I gained from the experience.

I learned a lot from est. First there was "The Anatomy of the Mind." Then there were all the lessons from the final Sunday night. I came to the understanding that "incompletes" are only incomplete if we allow them to be. It's the way we perceive them that counts. It would be impossible for us to complete everything in life, and probably not even wise. It is equally important to be able to release the "shoulds" when the time is right.

But the most important leap for me was that I had the courage to inform Mary Lou, the trainer, and my fellow trainees without hesitation or rancor that I was confident in my decision. I, who had always been so impressionable, was able to feel okay about standing up to my own convictions in the face of tremendous pressure, because I knew that what I was doing was right for *me*. The Mrs. Milquetoast who had allowed herself to be signed up for the training so easily, now, thanks to the training itself, was her own person. I had never respected myself so much.

23

B Y LATE 1982, I WAS riding high, empowered by my new-found ability to manage pain, as well as my thoughts about illness and the future. I was working full-time and studying part-time, taking courses that I enjoyed. I was more engaged in living than I had been since Sylvio died. My pain was under control. I was able to walk normally, I was doing my daily practice of deep relaxation, and I was seeing Lorraine once a week.

I was also as unrelentingly curious as ever. The only difference was the focus. Now I was reading everything I could get my hands on about alternative healing. I had become addicted.

I had also become addicted to positive thinking, to the great annoyance of my family and friends. At the time, I believed that I could control my thoughts, though I later learned that sheer dint of effort was not enough to change them. I now focus on my *reactions* to thoughts instead of the thoughts themselves.

Nevertheless, three decades ago I was getting great comfort from audio tapes with uplifting messages, which I would listen to for hours, especially during deep relaxation.[39] The people on the tapes gave voice to empowering thoughts like:

"I am a problem-solving mechanism. I am built to solve problems."

And relaxing thoughts that would guide my breathing and teach me to love my body, such as:

"Thank your feet for the wonderful job they do."

My thirst for self-help books was unquenchable. I routinely checked the shelves at the bookstore around the corner from my house—the famous Kramerbooks & Afterwords[40]—and pored through mail-order catalogs of publishers' overstock. One title that caught my eye was Nelson Hendler's *Coping with Chronic Pain*.[41] I sent for it, and when it arrived, I dove in immediately and read it from cover to cover.

While pain was no longer an issue for me, the book gave me an understanding of the subject that would have been extremely helpful two years earlier. It would have saved me a lot of anguish and time lost from living. Even so, it helped me a lot in my continuing recovery, and the book was to play an unintended role in my future.

Despite all I had been through, I had never understood the concept of *chronic* pain. To me, pain was pain. If asked, I would have said that acute pain is sharp, isolated, and severe (as, for example, with a sprained ankle) and chronic pain is duller, more generalized, and doesn't go away easily. According to Hendler, the difference is critical. He explains that chronic pain is a complicated condition. It can be just as intense and severe, but because it's more complex, it requires more and different tools than those used to treat acute pain.

I began to understand. All pain starts out the same—with a trigger, like an uncomfortable shoe, an encounter with a car door, or a body part that's acting up. In the beginning, all pain is acute. But acute pain is limited. To look at it backwards, if it went away within two months, whether with treatment or on its own, it was acute. Once it sets in over time, it crosses the line and becomes chronic.

Of course, that's what I had had two years earlier. I had fought against the term *chronic* because I thought that doctors would pay less attention and be more likely to blame it on the female personality or "psychogenic" causes. I didn't want to be dismissed. Hendler made me feel much better about my past situation when he emphasized that chronic pain is very real.

What makes it different is that, as time passes, other physical, mental, and emotional processes come into play and settle into complex patterns that cloud the original cause and ultimately take on a life of their own. The picture gets even murkier if the original pain is referred from its source. I saw myself once again. My hip pain was referred from the spine. And I had been going through a galaxy of mental and emotional processes. There was my grieving for Sylvio, my reactions to metastasis, my focus on death, my frustration with the doctors' uncertainty, my anxiety over becoming disabled, and of course the pain itself. None of these issues was anything to be ashamed of. There was a certain logic to all of them. The confirmation that I hadn't done anything "wrong" was very freeing.

I could certainly relate to Hendler's discussion of how doctors often respond to patients with chronic pain. Since they are accustomed to finding the cause of acute pain, when they can't find a cause, they assume that the patient is either not cooperating or suffering from an overactive imagination—or worse. This was what happened to me. It was the hardest part of my ordeal: not being heard or taken seriously. By the time my pain had become chronic, it required more tools than most doctors knew how to use. It wasn't their fault, and it wasn't mine. Finally, someone understood the frustration I had gone through! I was relieved that I was not the only one who had had to face doubting doctors.

I had also been right to avoid painkillers. Hendler emphasizes that pain pills can easily be misused in chronic pain and he doesn't recommend them. Their main role is to mask the pain until the body can heal itself. They don't work with chronic pain because there are too many factors to address. Addiction happens because more medicine is added on the false assumption that the previous dose wasn't enough. I might add, from my own experience, that the crash that comes when relief ends and the pain comes back is crazy-making, or at least it was for me. That's what happened the night I tried to kill myself.

Hendler emphasizes that a combination of long-term approaches is needed—and most important, steady commitment on the part of the patient. That reminded me of my orthopedist, who had told me the same thing. He had gotten me started on several approaches at the same time and had warned me that I needed to be patient. Now I saw how wise he had been.

Another new concept for me was that Hendler considers chronic pain a disease in itself, not a symptom of something else. It has more than one cause and it has a psychological component (like most disease, I have come to learn). He offers a number of approaches that can be used to treat it, including surgery, nerve blocks, electrical stimulators, physical therapy, exercise, psychotherapy, biofeedback (yes!), hypnosis, acupuncture, behavior modification, and other kinds of medication— antidepressants, for example. The treatment plan can enlist all or any of the approaches mentioned above, tailored to the circumstances. When I read this, at first I wished that I could have found a doctor like Hendler to orchestrate my case—and then I realized that I had become my own doctor. My inner "maestro" had done the job.

Hendler describes eight types of pain and four types of patients: the Coper, the Exaggerator, the Moper, and the Malingerer. I took the test to find my type, rating myself the way I was when I was suffering the most. I turned out to be an Exaggerator. After my comeback, I was a Coper. And by the time I became a Coper, my pain was on its way out.

Even though Dr. Hendler himself is trained as a psychiatrist, his reference to one-on-one psychotherapy is quite brief. He merely suggests in general terms that psychotherapy may help to reveal how chronic pain fits into the patient's life, identify emotional needs, and guide the patient in finding solutions to the problem.

His mention of emotional needs took me back to Carl Simonton and the idea that there may be benefits in being sick that patients are not consciously aware of. I had thought about this with cancer, but for the first time I applied the same concept to my pain and wondered if I had been holding onto it for some reason. I can understand that this idea would be unthinkable to many chronic pain sufferers, but I am a deep-sea diver in the ocean of the psyche. I started thinking of reasons why I might not have been ready to release my pain. Was it a distraction to keep me from thinking about Sylvio? Was I punishing myself for his death? My grandfather's? My child's? Was I reluctant to move forward? Or was it simply a cry for help? It could have been all or any of these. At the very least, I realized how there could be deeper layers to chronic pain that add to the burden and further complicate the chances of finding relief. Simply looking at these questions, without exploring the answers, took me another step forward on my journey.

After reading the book, I concluded that I was already coping pretty well. I thought I deserved a diploma. I didn't realize that countless other lessons still lay in store.

Part VI

Round Three

24

T HEY SAY THAT "GOD WRITES straight with crooked lines." Reading Nelson Hendler's *Coping with Chronic Pain* was the first step in a chain of events that was about to unfold.

I might have accepted my "diploma" as a certified Coper, digested the new insights, and moved on. But I couldn't leave well enough alone. The book had reawakened my nagging desire for more information. I was encouraged by Hendler's thoroughness, his open mind, and his explanation why most doctors don't understand chronic pain. From his book, I understood that he had had very good success in identifying the source of his patients' pain, based on his own experience and with the help of a network of specialists that he sent them to. If he didn't have the answer himself, he knew the right place to go. I decided that I had one more chance to get to the bottom of what had happened in my spine. Was it cancer? Or if it wasn't, what was it?

From the dust jacket, I already knew that Dr. Hendler was based in Stevenson, Maryland. I looked up Stevenson and learned that it was little more than a crossroads in rural Maryland northwest of Baltimore. It was 60 miles away. Unfazed by the trek, I made an appointment to see him.

The Mensana Clinic [42] for treating chronic pain was housed in a fin-de-siècle mansion overlooking rolling farmland in Greenspring Valley. A row of majestic two-story columns towered over the entrance. When I walked into the foyer, I was met by a sweeping staircase and, on each side of the foyer, enormous paneled rooms with hunting trophies on the walls. Polished wood floors were covered in oriental rugs and animal pelts. One room had a giant pair of elephant tusks framing the fireplace.[43] Dr. Hendler greeted me and explained that the space was for groups of patients, who sometimes stayed there on a residential basis. I remember feeling glad that I was not a candidate, since treatment for chronic pain was no longer on my agenda.

The tusks made me shudder. Still, I was on a mission to get answers. My hopes rose when Dr. Hendler pressed his finger directly on the sore spot on my L5 vertebra and triggered a piercing pain that radiated to the hip. I was impressed that he knew to go straight to the spot and make my hip hurt. I felt vindicated that he had been able to reproduce the pain—something that no other doctor had tried to do.

We talked about whether it might have been arthritis, and he said he didn't think it was. He ordered a series of blood tests to rule out arthritis and some other conditions. I mentioned that in my own very small universe I had noticed that people who had cancer didn't usually get arthritis and vice versa. This had been true in my biological family. He nodded:

"Smart girl!

"With arthritis, the immune system is overactive. It has turned against the body it is supposed to protect. In cancer, on the other hand, the immune system is weak; it has been overpowered and is struggling to do its job."

I was flattered that he validated my idea. I felt respected instead of diminished. We agreed on so many things. How could I not like him? I was still thinking about the elephant tusks.

At my second appointment, he reviewed the results of the blood tests. None of them showed signs of the conditions he was testing for, including arthritis. His next step was to order a complete workup at Johns Hopkins Hospital.

The word in those days was that after a patient had tried all other options, Johns Hopkins was the last place to go. "They've taken him to Baltimore," people would say in hushed tones, with a mix of sadness and hope. I was dazzled by its reputation and willing to embark on a new battery of tests if that's what it took to finally unlock the mysteries surrounding the lesion in my spine. Cost was not an issue. My health insurance—the same insurance that kept me chained to my employer—would pay for everything.

At Hopkins, I met with the doctor who was going to coordinate my case. He sent me for consultations and tests in various services around the hospital over a period of a couple of weeks. Each time, I drove up from Washington.

After numerous tests, I came back to review the results with the main doctor. He informed me that the place on my spine was merely arthritis (which I have had no other sign of to this day). I mentioned that I had been trained in biofeedback and had used deep relaxation to overcome pain, and he dismissed it out of hand.

"That's all a crock! You're wasting your time."

I was disappointed in the outcome, disappointed in the doctor's attitude, and disappointed in Johns Hopkins. I said good-bye to him and started walking down the hall toward the exit. I had almost reached the door when he came running after me. He had just received the report from my mammogram, the one result we hadn't discussed. It showed a well-defined lump in my left breast, right underneath the nipple.

Now he was interested.

With no time to think. I followed him back to his office. His secretary set up an appointment at the cancer polyclinic, where a team of doctors would develop a treatment plan. It was explained to me that the clinic had specialists in all the latest approaches and they would work together to come up with the best plan for me.

And so there I was: on track to being treated for a cancer that 15 minutes earlier I didn't even know I had.

As I left, I was still thinking about my spine. If I thought at all about the new lump in my other breast, I wasn't worried. It was just a minor inconvenience.

But I was soon to discover that part of me was still invested in a lifelong habit of relying on doctors. When faced with a real issue, I was conflicted. I was comforted by the idea of working with the polyclinic. "The best plan for me" sounded more personalized than the previous clinic with the big numbers on the wall. It gave me a sense of security. The "old Muriel" who wanted answers and treatment was alive and well. I had fallen into lock step with the "system."

In fact, I was so locked in that it didn't occur to me to go back to Dr. Purcell or Dr. Laird. I was on auto-pilot, simply following directions.

On the drive home, the "new Muriel" began to wake up. Once again, my craving for answers and solutions was at odds with my feelings about radiation, surgery, and chemotherapy. I had forgotten that I hated and/or disapproved of all the standard treatments for cancer. There was almost nothing the clinic—the "burn-slash-and-poison team"—could do for me that I would have wanted to have done.

I remembered my faith in biofeedback and the power of the human mind. The only problem was that I couldn't figure out how to apply my new beliefs to a known lump in my breast. I was confused. I didn't know which way to turn, or even if I had an alternative. My mind kept spinning on multiple tracks.

I finally concluded that a biopsy was inevitable. I told myself that without basic information about the tumor, I wouldn't be able to make wise decisions. That seemed to make sense. At my next appointment with the oncologist, I consented to a biopsy, but I made no other commitments.

When I met with the surgeon, I got him to promise that he would only do a biopsy. Just to make sure, I insisted on being awake during the operation, regardless of the pain. The surgeon numbed my breast with local anesthesia. His movements with the knife seared all the way through me, but I invoked the techniques I had learned to block out the pain. I watched as he cut a circle around the perimeter of the areola—like a can opener.

Afterwards, the surgeon came to see me in my hospital room and told me the lump had been cancerous, but he was confident he had "gotten it all." He said he thought I could manage without any further treatment. I was delighted.

However, the experts at the polyclinic didn't agree. When I came back to meet with the oncologist, he proposed a full mastectomy, radiation, and chemotherapy.

Mastectomy!!!?!!

The biopsy was reasonable, but that was all the surgery I was prepared to go along with. I said I wasn't ready to consider it. He told me I had no choice. Well, . . . at the very least, I would have to have radiation and chemo. I said I would need to think about what I wanted to do. I couldn't make a decision on the spot.

My friend Ruth had been kind enough to give me a ride that day and keep me company. After my appointment, I reported to her what had transpired and the decisions I was facing. Before heading back to Washington, we took a break and had lunch at the Inner Harbor. Throughout the meal, I kept surreptitiously feeling my breast to make sure it was still here. It was nice and intact. I knew it was pretty, unlike the other one, which was scarred and misshapen. I couldn't imagine myself without it. I felt as if it was the last tangible link to my feminine identity. More important, it was *me*. I didn't see it as a body part, but rather as part of the whole. I decided there and then that I was going to keep it. I told Ruth:

"I've made up my mind. I'm not going to have the mastectomy."

That left radiation and chemo still on the table. I explained the options to Ruth. Radiation would be daily for six weeks. Even chemo required frequent visits to the clinic. While I had come this far, already burning a rut in the Baltimore-Washington Parkway, I wasn't prepared to make so many frequent trips, especially if I was under the weather with the treatment.

Ruth volunteered to drive me up. I could hardly believe her generosity. I was really touched. I thanked her for her incredible offer, but I knew it didn't make sense.

At my next appointment with the oncologist, I explained to him that I couldn't sustain the commute for follow-up treatment. He accepted my decision, and we decided that my file would be sent to an oncologist that he recommended in Washington.

My new bout with breast cancer upstaged my pursuit for answers about my spine. With the diagnosis of arthritis from Hopkins, I lost interest in seeing Dr. Hendler. Once and for all I gave up trying to find the cause of the mysterious lesion. I had a new focus.

25

I WASN'T THE LEAST BIT WORRIED about my prognosis with the new lump. I was confident that the cancer didn't have any power over me. I kept remembering that the surgeon had said I probably didn't need any further treatment. The problem had been solved as far as I was concerned. I never took the idea of further treatment very seriously. That was the "new Muriel" speaking. However, the "old Muriel" was still in the picture. I wasn't afraid of cancer any more, and I didn't want treatment, but I wasn't quite ready for the unknown.

So I went along with the plan to get treatment in Washington. The idea of seeing an entirely different team of doctors made the decision easier.

The new oncologist turned out to be as doggedly determined as Dr. Purcell had been relaxed and low-key. He requested more tests and a series of nuclear medicine studies, including yet another bone scan—my ninth, and what would turn out to be my last. Like the doctors at Hopkins, he, too, wanted a full mastectomy, radiation, and chemotherapy. He outlined his treatment plan as I sat on his examining table, draped and half-naked underneath. I felt vulnerable, and the options he was proposing were just as overwhelming in Washington as they had been in Baltimore. I heard myself saying:

"Would you mind if I got dressed and we talked in your office?"

He seemed rather surprised, but he honored my request. I'm proud of that little moment. I was learning to stand up for myself and not be pushed around by men in white coats. But even speaking with him in his office with my clothes on, I was not happy with what he had to say. Once again I was offered the same choices that I had been resisting.

I was now seriously worried about what I had gotten myself into. At Hopkins, I had the choice of not driving up to Baltimore. Here at home, I felt that I had no exit. Everyone knew where I lived. Though I wasn't consciously aware of it, I think I had a deep-seated fear that if I didn't do what the doctors told me to, they could come and get me, the way the est people had. I had read in the paper about court cases where a judge imposed treatment.

I negotiated with the oncologist. I talked him out of a mastectomy and chemotherapy, but I agreed to do radiation. He said it was the least I could get away with and still survive. I figured it was the price for my freedom, because I didn't know any other way to get out of the clutches of the treatment-crazy oncologists. At that point I was appreciating Dr. Purcell and wishing I had made the effort to go back to him.

By then it was February 1983. Not only was I facing another odd-numbered year, but the date was exactly six years after my first round of radiation. Even the weather was the same, with snow and slush under foot. I had a treatment planning session on Friday the 18th. The first step was to discuss the plan with the radiation oncologist. I waited for him in a cubicle, dressed in a paper gown. He walked in with my chart and reviewed his proposed plan. Cobalt-60 would be delivered in daily doses over the next six weeks, the same schedule I had had before. Then he said:

"Now I need to examine you. Stand up and take off the gown, please."

I had nothing on underneath except my panties, but I did as I was told. I stood there for at least a minute feeling completely exposed as he stared at me. He gradually moved closer until his lips were only a few inches from mine. Then he put the palms of both his hands on my waist, slid them up, and started fondling my breasts. It had happened so smoothly that at first I didn't realize what was going on. For a fleeting moment, it felt nice. Then I came to my senses and stiffened my body. He moved back.

I was speechless. I didn't know what to say or do. We finished our business, and I left. I can't say I was as outraged as I should have been, but I knew that what he did was an invasion of my privacy, unprofessional, and very wrong. I thought of reporting the incident, but I knew that no one would listen to me and he would deny it. He had me over a barrel: once again I would be typed as a hysterical woman with an empty life and a vivid imagination. I made a conscious decision to let the matter drop.

Preparations for treatment took place the following Tuesday. I only remember that one of the technicians tattooed little dots on my chest to mark the radiation field. She hadn't asked my permission, and I felt slightly violated, as if my right to make decisions about my body had been taken away from me. The tattoos became a metaphor, and I eventually paid good money to have them removed.

My treatments were scheduled for eight o'clock in the morning so that I could stop by on my way to work. I marked each weekday morning in my datebook with the entry: "Zap!"

The first treatment, on Wednesday, was uneventful.

The next day I arrived to find the radiation technicians tinkering with the cobalt machine. After a delay, they placed me on the table and continued to address their problem. Looking up, I could see that a tray was loose. It was the tray holding the lead shields that frame the treatment area and protect the rest of the body from radiation. They fussed with it for quite a while and finally secured it with masking tape. Yes, masking tape—as God is my witness. When they left the room, the vibration as they closed the door caused the tray to slump. Then suddenly a beam of blazing white light came boring directly into my right eye. It was coming through a small hole and felt stronger than looking directly into the sun. I screamed, but they couldn't hear me. I closed my eye and kept screaming. Meanwhile, the machine continued to go through its paces. When the round was over and the technicians came back in, I was livid and told them what had happened. They seemed sheepish but offered no apology. Worst of all, they showed no concern for me.

I went on to work, but by the end of the day the right side of my face and nose had turned bright red and my skin was tender to the touch.

When I woke up the next day, Friday, the side of my face was swollen and fiercely inflamed. It felt just like a burn one might get from a hot iron or a pan on the stove. At the hospital, I showed it to the technician and asked to have the doctor look at it. However, she insisted on doing my treatment first, arguing that it would be dangerous to skip a session—plus (probably her real reason) the dosage amounts would have to be recalculated. I felt I had no choice. When I got on the table, I could see that the tray had been fixed. And of course, there was no beam in my eye.

Afterwards, I saw the doctor and told him the story. He examined my face and said:

"You have some kind of infection there. You should see a dermatologist."

I was beyond rage. Not only was he denying responsibility, but he was dismissing my concerns and making me feel that I had imagined the entire event. Once again I wasn't being heard—the issue that has dogged me my entire life. Obviously I knew the difference between a burn and an infection, and I knew my situation was serious. It was clear that he was being dishonest and betraying his profession. I recalled the fondling incident and concluded that he was prepared to try to get away with whatever he could.

That evening my neighbor Schuyler dropped by and I showed her what had happened. She was so angry that she said:

"If you think you're going back to that place, you have another think coming. To make sure you don't, I'm going to bring my sleeping bag and spend the night right here," pointing to the floor next to the front door.

I assured her that nothing was going to happen over the week-end. That evening, I covered the damage with makeup and went to the movies on a date. "Gandhi" was playing on a wide screen with surround sound, and as I watched the movie, I felt the side of my face turn numb. I kept touching it and couldn't feel a thing. Then I realized it was *paralyzed*. I was terrified. The thought came to me in a flash of understanding:

"This doctor only cares about covering his backside. I can't place my health in his hands. The only person I can trust to take care of me is *me*."

There was no point in seeing another doctor. I wouldn't trust him, either; I knew that they would just cover for each other. There was no one else I could look to; I was in this alone. I thought of what Schuyler had said, and I remembered how Sylvio had begged me to stop radiation back in 1977. I finally understood that I had a choice. I didn't *have* to keep taking the treatments. The police weren't going to come after me. I could walk away. Yes, I could walk free!

Though it was late when I got home, I sat down and wrote a letter to the radiation oncologist saying that I was not coming back for the rest of my treatments. I kept a copy, which I still have.

The paralysis lasted for about two weeks. The skin on my face settled into a dark purplish-ashy blue—what my grandmother would have called *blae*. I covered it with makeup and managed as best I could. Some days I didn't go to work and had to miss my classes. Eventually the feeling in my skin returned to normal and the strange color subsided.

Many years later, I lost more than half my sight from glaucoma in the affected eye, although the other eye continues to be normal. I have wondered if my damaged vision was a late effect of this overexposure to radiation.

The doctor responded to my letter and told me that my survival was threatened if I didn't come back and complete my treatments. The other oncologist got word of my rebellious act and called me at my office. If I wasn't going to have radiation, he said, I had to agree to some other treatment:

"I've decided that the only safe thing to do is take off both your breasts and make you flat."

I was horrified. And I knew better. I knew that I didn't need to have both breasts removed. I told him:

"I'm sorry, but I'm not interested in discussing that."

"Of course," he said, "it was insensitive of me to bring it up on the phone. Please come and see me in my office."

I replied:

"No, I mean it. I'm not interested in discussing it."

I hung up politely, and I never made an appointment to see him. I didn't answer the letter from the radiation oncologist, either. I never saw either of them, or in fact any other oncologist, again.

I decided there and then that if my breast cancer was ever to return in the future, I would refuse treatment. Thus, there was no point in looking for shadows on mammograms. Instead, I would stay well and practice my principles. Rather than being cut into pieces, zapped with radiation, and tied to tubes of poison, I would spend whatever time was left enjoying life to the fullest.

It took that one last lump to reinforce all I had learned.

Part VII

Walking Free

26

I CAN THANK EST FOR TEACHING me to walk away when I knew the time was right. I'm not talking about the training—which had its merits—but about the moment when I knew it was time to go home and the estians chased me all the way back to my house in an effort to get me to return. Standing up to their stubborn pressure taught me to trust my own wisdom in the face of strong opposition. It was the cauldron that turned my determination into steel. It gave me the strength to say "no" to the cancer establishment and walk away when I finally came to believe that the treatments were doing me more harm than good.

It wasn't as if I walked away from radiation with nothing to take its place. I had other tools that I trusted. I was religiously committed to deep relaxation, biofeedback, imagery, and the messages on tape that I found so empowering, and I knew I would continue to follow these practices on a daily basis. My trump card was that I was no longer afraid of cancer. Thanks to the Simontons, I had come to understand that it was part of me, and I couldn't cure it by fighting it. The "war on cancer" was a war against my own body, and therefore unwinnable. I was starting to see cancer as the best thing that had ever happened to me, because it had taught me so much. It had been the trigger that launched me on a path of total change.

Though I had walked away from doctors and hospitals, I was still open to therapies, as long as they were gentle and designed to get my body to heal itself.

Schuyler, my neighbor who had urged me to quit radiation, had a couple of alternatives up her sleeve: homeopathy and anthroposophy.[44] I had heard about homeopathy from my Norwegian family and had dabbled in it a little. Through my Norwegian ties I had also heard of anthroposophy and its founder, Rudolf Steiner.[45] My father's sister Astrid was a devotee and had spent time living in an anthroposophical community. She was the only one of my five Norwegian aunts who reached out to me. She sent me delightful, imaginative gifts when I was a child, and when I was older, she wrote to me about Steiner. I thought of him as a strongly spiritual philosopher and a leader in bringing about social change. I admired his work in the field of education, seen today in the Waldorf schools, and I was also aware that he had been one of the early promoters of organic farming. But I didn't know anything about anthroposophical medicine. Thanks to Aunt Astrid, I was prepared to look into it.

I was surprised to find out that anthroposophical medicine is well established throughout the world, especially in Europe, with its own treatment centers and medical schools. I learned that the system is founded on the belief that spiritual awareness is the basis of all health. [46] Schuyler gave me an English translation of one of Steiner's medical treatises to read, but I have to confess, I found it impossible to follow. That did not diminish my respect for him.

Steiner saw the mistletoe plant as a metaphor for cancer, and it became the basis for development of the cancer therapy known as Iscador®. [47]

Schuyler, with the help of her father, was able to find a doctor in the Washington area who was willing to help me obtain Iscador and oversee my treatment. He was both an M.D. and a homeopath.

The doctor found the address for the Institut Hiscia in Germany and wrote to them to find out about using Iscador. Enclosed with their answer was a disc of special blotting paper and instructions for taking a sample of my blood. They explained that the findings from the blood test would be used to prescribe my dosing schedule. He blotted a sample of my blood onto the paper and returned it to them, and the analysis that came back was uncanny. From that dried spot of blood that had traveled across the Atlantic in an ordinary envelope, they were able to reconstruct my medical history, including an earlier ovarian cyst, the first breast lump, the lesion on my spine (so there really *was* something there!), and then the second lump. They were now in a position to prescribe.

The box that arrived from Germany contained neat rows of single-dose vials in graduated sizes. The doctor taught me how to inject myself, and I kept up the treatment for the entire course, which lasted about 18 months, if I remember correctly. He saw me every month or so and also prescribed homeopathic remedies.

I have no way of knowing if the Iscador "worked," or how much the other remedies helped, but I have always believed that I chose the right things to do. Certainly my overall health kept getting better.

By the time I finished with Iscador, I was walking "free"— absolutely free of pain, and more free of guilt and anxiety than I had ever been. I knew that pain and suffering are no more or less than what I make of them. I also came to understand that the rules that apply to cancer also apply to the rest of my life. I saw that the feelings I had had over the years were really just reactions to *thoughts* I had attached to them. I began to enjoy the freedom of not buying into thoughts that made me uncomfortable and complicated my life. At the time, I equated this to "positive thinking." However, as I learned more, I saw some of the limitations of positive thinking and the impossibility of "controlling" my thoughts. Eventually I realized that I was engaged in a lifelong process of discovering ways to respond to my feelings that make my life richer and more empowering.

I continued to grieve for Sylvio. He left a void that will never be filled. But he lives on in my dreams, even today. He comes to me in my sleep, and he usually says:

"You thought I was gone, didn't you? You should have trusted me. Of course I was coming back."

He lets me believe he will be with me forever. I look forward to the comfort of those dreams and to the day when I will reunite with him once and for all.

Of course I can still get impatient and frustrated; I sometimes allow myself to feel wounded; I feel devastated when dear friends die; I can be overwhelmed by challenges; I have had crises that seemed beyond my control; and I have had physical limitations to deal with. But these experiences no longer hurt. I know that each one turns out to be a catalyst that opens up a new phase of learning and understanding—the more intense the experience, the more valuable the lesson. The sooner I recognize them as opportunities, the more quickly they shift. These are the times when I open up and discover new worlds. I have learned that when I think I have mastered what I need to know, it's always a sure sign that I have a lot more to learn.

So "walking free" was the beginning of a new journey, a fresh start in life.

27

I LIKE TO THINK OF MY graduate degrees as byproducts of a much higher education in a field I had not set out to major in—namely, unconditional love.

When I went back to school in 1977 and started taking courses in linguistics again, I didn't have a focus, and I wasn't even sure I wanted a degree. After Sylvio died, I had even less motivation, but I knew that going to school provided me with healthy structure in difficult times.

I hesitated to make a commitment for a number of reasons. I didn't see the benefit of a graduate degree because I already had a job, and I knew I could never work anywhere else. The courses I was taking, though their titles were intriguing, didn't actually satisfy my curiosity about language. But most important, and much deeper, I had long-standing insecurities that had to do with Aunt Muriel. As her namesake, I was always measuring myself against her—and then trying not to. She already had her Ph.D. by the time I was born, and I had mixed feelings about what her success represented to me.

In fact, Aunt Muriel had many stripes on her sleeve. She was inducted into Phi Beta Kappa as an undergraduate at Wellesley College; she had a master's degree in psychology from Stanford University; and she earned her Ph.D. from Johns Hopkins University in a day when few women even went to graduate school. She was well known, had won a number of awards, and was acquainted with some very interesting people.

When I was finishing high school, I never doubted that I would go on to get an undergraduate degree. But I had always been leery of any decision that would make me feel as if I was competing with Aunt Muriel. I definitely didn't want to try something that she was good at and fail. When I applied to colleges and universities, I made certain that they didn't have a chapter of Phi Beta Kappa. I would ask myself: "What if I don't make it?"

Comparisons had haunted our relationship since I was a child. As much as I compared myself to her, I also felt that she was trying to put me down so that she could shine. If I came home with good grades, she would fetch her awards and diplomas, spread them out on the dining room table, and tell me about each one and how important it was. If she was trying to inspire me, that's not the message I got.

My grandmother, who lived with us, worshipped the ground she walked on and never ceased to remind Mother and me what an important and successful woman she was. In the same breath, my grandmother would disparage my mother and suggest that she was incompetent. Mother was actually very smart. However, my grandmother and her siblings had type-cast her from childhood as a dummy. They ignored or made fun of her and gave her the dirty work to do. Identifying with my mother, I resented the way they ran her down and lavished praise on my aunt.

So, did I really want to follow in Aunt Muriel's footsteps and get a Ph.D.? What would her reaction be? Was I invading her domain? Did I want to take the chance and show her I was as good as she was? And always the big one: What if I tried and failed? These questions brought up a lot of fears, and I didn't know the answers. My ambivalence about Aunt Muriel was being reflected in my commitment to my studies. I often thought of walking away from the whole thing.

When I went back to Georgetown in 1977, Aunt Muriel was still quite hale and hearty. She was a consultant to an association of toymakers and was traveling a lot. But after Margaret Mead's death, she began to decline noticeably. Although she was articulate, she started to do strange things, like hiding herself—once, for example, on the floor of the rear seat of the car. She was no longer the formidable power that I had always imagined her to be, but in my mind, she continued to represent something I could never be as good as.

Still, as indecisive as I was, I kept on taking courses in linguistics at Georgetown. If they weren't offered in the evening, I would use annual leave or flextime hours during the day. The tuition came from various sources: the "found" money in my student account, education grants provided by my office, and my own pocket.

Linguistics is a very broad field. If I was going to keep on studying, the time came when I had to settle on an area of concentration. Since my office was experimenting with machine translation, I started out in computational linguistics. I accumulated enough credits for the master's degree in linguistics, but I had to face the fact that the computational area was not my cup of tea. I didn't have the patience to write computer programs. I don't have much patience anyway, and waiting for a printout the next day to see if my program had worked—and it usually hadn't—demanded a level of commitment far beyond any interest I had in the subject. So I switched to theoretical linguistics, hoping to find answers to how language works. The literature we were supposed to read was incomprehensible (to me, at least), and none of the theories satisfied me. The trees and other diagrams all seemed unidimensional. I see language as a multidimensional process in which many intentions are being expressed at the same time.

I finally started to find the answers I was looking for when I took a seminar in functional linguistics, which provided explanations that were very satisfying to me.[48] My teacher in discourse analysis, Deborah Schiffrin, was especially helpful, and it was Debbie who finally set me on my academic path. I finally found purpose, and I got serious about the Ph.D.

As my enthusiasm gained momentum, I stepped up my program until I accumulated enough of the right kind of credits.

When I finally completed my classwork, I was 50 years old and I had taken 30 courses in linguistics, far more than the required 18. Of course, I knew even then that education is never wasted. What I learned is part of who I am today.

The next step was the dissertation itself. By that time I knew that I wanted to do my research on discourse features in translation. Debbie accepted to be my mentor. She took pains to understand what I wanted to do with my topic, and she always found time to give me excellent guidance. She had a way of heading me in the right direction and getting me to come up with my own solutions. In response to her suggestions, as well as input from my other two committee members, I rewrote my first chapter 24 times. Each rewrite gave me sharper focus, which carried through to the rest of the project.

In addition to my committee, a group of students in the sociolinguistics program formed a dissertation support group, and they invited me to join. I had never had the experience of people going the extra mile to help someone else succeed. We met once a week, and in between we made ourselves available to listen to each other's challenges and come up with suggestions. Nearly everyone graduated in record time. I learned a lot from these classmates, but the most important lesson was the power of mutual support.

Writing the dissertation took about 15 months. In the end, my opus[49] came to 578 pages, and I had over 300 references in the bibliography. My committee never commented on the length, but I'm sure they had better things to do with their time. Keeping things consistent over so many pages was a major challenge.

Graduation day finally arrived, and I received my diploma on May 24, 1985. My mother came to the ceremony. By that time she was 87. She was proud of me, as I was of her.

Although graduation was nice, if ever there was a shining hour in my life, it was the awards ceremony at my office. Every year the Personnel Department sponsored an event to recognize employees for their years of service. The program also included acknowledgment of a few other staff accomplishments, including degrees earned with assistance from the department's training and education grants. The ceremony was held in the large auditorium and most of the seats were filled, so there must have been at least a hundred people. It was a low-energy affair, with light sprinkles of applause as people walked to the stage to get their awards. The "award" in the case of the education grants was just a piece of paper, and I don't even remember what it looked like. But I do remember the reaction when my name was called. People stood up, and the applause was thunderous. It kept on going as I made my way to the stage and I thought it was never going to end. I knew it was an acknowledgment of all I had gone through to get to that point, not just the degree. I was shocked to realize that so many people cared about me.

For the next few years I kept on going like the Energizer Bunny. I had so much momentum from the research I had been doing that I kept peeling off ideas and turning them into articles, some of which were published in peer-reviewed journals. I wrote on other translation-related topics as well, and by the time my writing stint ended, I had a list of about fifty publications.[50]

The degree actually did lead to a promotion at work. My half-time job in 1979 eventually morphed into a position as head of Spanish and English Translation Services, which included supervising the development and use of machine translation.

The great irony was that, while others recognized my accomplishments, Aunt Muriel never did. By the time I graduated, she was 94 and suffering from senile dementia. I told her about my degree and she smiled, but she never showed that she understood. On the contrary, she had become obsessed with her own Ph.D. She kept the leather-framed diploma propped up on a shelf across from her bed so that she could see it at all times. When I visited her, the first thing she would do was point to it and beam, and throughout the visit she would keep interrupting to go back and point to it again. In fact, her degree was one of the few subjects on which she was lucid. Otherwise, I would usually come in and find her sitting on the edge of her bed staring into space and singing the first bars of the "Alphabet Song" over and over again:

"A-B-C-D-E-F-G . . . H- I-J-K-LMNOP . . . A-B-C-D-E-F-G . . . H- I-J-K-LMNOP . . . A-B-C-D-E-F-G . . . H- I-J-K-LMNOP . . . "

In her mind, Aunt Muriel saw two of everything. For example, a young friend went to visit her with her child, and Aunt Muriel reported that "two ladies" had come with "their children." My dog Sunshine became two dogs, and Gracelita, the woman who took her meals to her, was also two people. At first her reports confused me, until I realized that everything was doubled. I never found a medical explanation. This doubling applied to new experiences, but many of her old memories remained intact.

In my case, she not only saw two of me, but she also thought of me as two very different people. It turned out to be a convenient strategy for dealing with her mixed feelings. Clearly, she hated one of us and loved the other. The latter Muriel visited her daily, saw that she was taken care of, and took her to doctor appointments and the Emergency Room. She was very sweet to that Muriel. She would share with her the dark feelings she harbored toward the other Muriel, adding the surname *Vasconcellos*—with her upper lip slightly curled. Sometimes she would ask for news about Muriel *Vasconcellos,* and I would keep a straight face and give her a brief update. This happened once in my mother's presence. Mother, who had a mischievous streak and little patience with her sister, decided to make a game of it and tried to make me laugh. At one point she said:

"Dear, when you see her, be sure to tell her that Aunt Muriel was asking for her."

I gave her a dirty look and kept up the pretense with my aunt.

So it wasn't just my imagination that Aunt Muriel struggled with ungenerous feelings toward me. My nose for deception when I was growing up had been spot on. It gave me some confidence to know that my reading of our relationship had been accurate and I wasn't a bad person for questioning her feelings toward me. Second, somewhere inside, she had the capacity to love me. She was just as conflicted as I was. Now I had options to choose from. I could give power to her anger and resentment, or I could believe that she loved me. I decided to go with the latter. I stopped worrying about what she thought of the other Muriel. I also realized that it was time for me to open up *my* heart as well. In fact, it became clear that if I didn't, she was going to continue being a stone in my life, whether she was still on the planet or had passed on. I got in touch with the feeling of her loving me and cherished it. Feeling her love enabled me to feel mine for her. We became very close.

During my visits, she began to share her secrets. She confessed that she had cheated in her classes at Johns Hopkins. Moreover, she had copied a classmate's work in her dissertation. Her dissertation disappeared after she deposited it, and when it was found, many of the sheets had been torn out by a classmate who was obviously quite angry at her. She almost didn't graduate. If these stories were true, it's surprising that she *did* graduate. It's also very sad. It would mean that for all her adult life she must have felt she was a fake. It would also mean that I had been competing with an ideal that never existed.

In my living room bookcase I have two editions of the *Dictionary of International Biography,* one dated 1975[51] and the other, 1990/91.[52] There used to be many directories of this kind, modeled after the big *Who's Who*. My aunt's name is found in the 1975 edition. I inherited her copy. I bought the 1990/91 edition to keep it company, because that's where *my* name appears. Did I try to emulate her? Did I try to compete with her? Is my 1990/91 listing intended to "show her" something, even if she will never see it? I still don't know the answers to these questions. What I have learned is that it truly doesn't matter. What matters is that in the last two years of her life, I dropped my guard and found that I really did love her. Instead of resenting her success, I can see it as a legacy to be proud of. The books are simply a reminder of this important lesson.

In the end, I believe that that's what my higher education was all about. My greatest reward was not the sheepskin or the better job; it was my first taste of truly unconditional love.

28

A UNT MURIEL'S DETERIORATION BEGAN TO be evident back in 1980.
She would get lost when she was driving and forget her way
home, and she caused three serious accidents with the car. One
time she barreled straight into the side of the house, demolishing
the guest bathroom where a visitor had been sitting on the toilet
barely a minute before. There were many other signs of dementia
as well. The winter of 1983-1984 brought matters to a head. There
was no doubt that our family had a problem.

By that time Aunt Muriel was 92 and Mother was soon to
turn 86.

Christmas 1983 never happened. The house, located on
bottomland with steep hills on each side, was surrounded by a
thick sheet of ice. Roads were closed for miles around, and even
the main highway was impassable. Then the pipes froze. For
over a week these two old ladies had no water and were forced to
suffer temperatures below freezing inside the house. The phone
lines were open, so I stayed in touch, but there was nothing I
could do.

Everything pointed to the same conclusion: it was time for
them to move. They couldn't spend another winter in such an
isolated situation.

During a phone call in January, Mother told me that she was
very sick. In all the years, it was the only time I had ever heard
her complain. I knew her condition had to be serious. I checked
in every day and called her doctor to ask him to follow up. After
about a week she called to say that she needed to get to the

hospital. I contacted her doctor again, and he arranged to have an ambulance pick her up.

The nurses told me later that when she arrived she looked as if she was 12 months pregnant. Two days went by before the doctors figured out she had a ruptured appendix—very rare in a person her age and something they hadn't thought to look for. By then, she had massive peritonitis; her body was flooded with a deadly infection. When I got there, she was being taken to the Operating Room. Afterwards, the surgeon told me that her heart had stopped before they began to give her anesthesia. They were able to resuscitate her and get on with the procedure, which was the only hope of saving her life. It was a miracle she survived.

Later she told me:

"I died while I was on the operating table. But I decided to come back, because I couldn't leave you with this mess on your hands."

The "mess" she was referring to was the urgent need to close the house in the country and find a place, or places, for the two of them to live. She told me about her near-death experience. It had been an indescribably wonderful feeling, she said. She felt herself being pulled toward a light, until she suddenly remembered that she still had a job to do and felt herself "come back" with a thud. Later she said more than once that it would have been easier to yield to the force that was pulling her away. She would ask me for reassurance that her effort to come back was appreciated:

"Did I do the right thing?"

I loved her very much and was delighted to have her with me, so it was easy for me to reassure her that her effort had been worth it. After the surgery, she was in Intensive Care for several days, part of that time in a haze, unable to talk rationally. When she could finally form sentences, the first thing she said was:

"Dear, I'm going to live with you."

I was overjoyed. Since I was a child, I had wanted to have her to myself, and it always seemed as if someone—usually my aunt—was in the way. I went to Woodward & Lothrop and bought her a "trousseau" of new clothes. When she was discharged from the hospital, I brought her directly back to Washington. She needed nursing care, so for three months she stayed in a facility until she was well enough to come home with me.

That left Aunt Muriel alone in the house in Virginia. It was a dangerous situation, because she was forgetful and confused and still driving the car. I went to see her several times in an effort to resolve the situation. She refused to leave. Searching for a solution, I read a book on senile dementia, *The 36-Hour Day*,[53] which described Aunt Muriel's behavior to a T, and the words that popped up from the page for me were "you must intervene." The author, Dr. Peter Rabins, was at Johns Hopkins Hospital, and I phoned him to ask for his advice. He urged me to take action.

Still, all our efforts failed. I hired an attorney specialized in elder law. There was a matter of power of attorney, because she was incompetent to make decisions. Months went by. Mother and I were very worried. I mentioned the problem to my homeopath, and he said:

"You've come to the right place!"

He gave me a powdered remedy in a folded paper and told me to put it in a glass of fruit juice and give it to my aunt.

We were so desperate that we were ready to try anything. Mother believed she was the only one who could get Aunt Muriel to take the magic potion. Marshaling what little strength she had, she said she would go to the country and slip Aunt Muriel the "mickey." I drove her to the country and left her there. The next day, she poured the powder into a glass of orange juice and gave it to Aunt Muriel to drink. About two minutes later, Aunt Muriel turned into a lamb: she gave up her car keys and agreed to move out and put the house up for sale. I often wondered: was the remedy for real? Or did it simply relax our attachment to the outcome so that she no longer had anything to push against?

At first, Aunt Muriel stayed in an assisted living complex in Strasburg, Virginia, near the foothills of the Blue Ridge Mountains. She had her own ground floor apartment with a view of the mountains, and she could keep her dog. The place was intended for seniors with minimal needs. There was no communal dining room, but the staff checked on the residents daily to make sure they were all right, and there was a social worker on duty. We paid a woman to buy her groceries, clean the apartment, and fix some of her meals. We would go to see her on from time to time, and always on holidays.

Back in Washington, with my new housemate, I no longer had time to dwell on healing. In addition to closing and selling the place in the country and seeing that Mother had what she needed, I was working full-time during the day and writing my thesis in the evenings and on week-ends, with a deadline looming. In all this mix, the long hours of deep relaxation and biofeedback exercises fell by the wayside. The point of the exercises had been to combat my anxiety and reframe the negative messages I was sending myself. The program filled an important need when I started it, but now I was too busy to even think about myself. Rumination was a luxury I could no longer afford.

One of my classmates, Liisa, was coming to the house during the day to use my word processor for her thesis. She was good company for my mother. Her husband was a Chinese doctor, a very handsome fellow from Taiwan by the name of Lee Tsong Shong. He had spent many years in a Buddhist monastery, where he studied traditional Chinese medicine. He and Liisa had met in Brazil, and she called him "André." He had an other-worldly air about him. I often saw him studying ancient Chinese texts. A master of the pulse diagnosis, he knew how to read all the many qualities and characteristics and their infinite variations through his fingers.

Before long, André was giving me acupuncture. I had never had it before, and though I have seen several acupuncturists since then, the experience with him was unique. He carried his custom-made gold needles in a dark red velvet pouch. He rarely applied more than two, often only one, and it never went deep.[54] When he inserted it, I would feel a powerful electric current running through my entire body.

André's intention was to make me completely whole again. He wasn't focused on any symptoms in particular, or even on cancer. He explained that in Chinese medicine, cancer is a symptom of deeper dysfunction, and if the source of the problem isn't treated, removing the cancer will cause it to come back more aggressively and turn against other parts of the body. To address my deeper problems, he gave me herbs that he ordered directly from China—dried, but in their natural form. Big chunky things, in fascinating shapes and colors. Mother would cook them into a tea for me, following his strict instructions.

A couple of times my formerly famous hip would kink up and start to hurt, and André would whack the muscle with the edge of his hand in just the right place to release the tension, and the problem would go away. He also did a foot-and-calf massage that was great for circulation but hurt like crazy. In addition, he sent me to a massage therapist, Dallas, for weekly full-body massages. Like André, Dallas was one of a kind. He was a Presbyterian minister and held a degree in agronomy from Cornell University. He had spent most of his adult life as a missionary in Iran, where he learned to speak fluent Farsi and got involved in local farming activities. André taught him some Chinese massage techniques, and the two of them even traveled to Taiwan together so that Dallas could learn *real* foot massage. I had weekly massages with Dallas for many years.

My program had now settled into a routine: weekly massages with Dallas, biweekly biofeedback with Lorraine, and Iscador and homeopathy.

On the day of my graduation from Georgetown in May 1985, my car's rear axle snapped during the short drive home. I had hours to wait, and I started reading a book that I happened to have with me, *You Can Have It All*, by Arnold M. Patent. Picking it up on the day of my graduation was so serendipitous that it could not have been planned. I had just wrapped up a big phase of my life, and a new one was waiting for me.

Everything the author said had a clear ring of truth to it. For me, he had "cracked the code" and developed a simple set of principles that remind us of a loving Universe that supports us at all times in purposeful ways. I knew immediately that it was the system I had been looking for. As I understood Arnold's work at the time, *You Can Have It All* means that we have the power to create what we want. In fact, we can know what we really want if we look at what we already have, because we chose to be where we are. To unlock our potential, we start by embracing what we have. We tap into our power by releasing attachment to judgments and desired outcomes. The Universe has far more wonderful opportunities in store for us than we, as humans, can possibly imagine. We open to them by letting go.

The principles are kept alive through regular structured support group meetings in many parts of the world, where members of a large network support one another in releasing judgment and observing how the principles are working in their daily lives. I started meeting regularly with a group of interested friends, and that fall, when Arnold came to the Washington area, we attended his workshop. The workshop gave me an extended family, and the support group that grew out of it became my immediate family.

In the spring of 1987, three years after Mother's health crisis, the social worker at Aunt Muriel's senior living facility called me at my office to tell me that Aunt Muriel had been knocking on people's doors and handing out rolls of toilet paper that she had taken from a supply closet. Residents were complaining. The social worker said that she had to leave.

What to do? Mother and I had just moved to a larger house, still on Corcoran Street and less than a block away from my home of 19 years. Mother helped me pay for it. The arrangement was much better for her: she had her own apartment on the ground floor with a separate entrance and floor-to-ceiling mullioned windows across the back giving onto a patio and garden. I had the two floors above. Mother didn't want Aunt Muriel to move in with us. With good reason. Aunt Muriel was constantly agitated, and it was exhausting to be around her. She could think up the most outlandish things to do, and you always had to be a close step behind her. There was a vacant basement apartment for rent across the street in a large old brownstone townhouse, and we moved her there. With her government pension, I was able to pay her rent and hire a young Brazilian woman, Gracelita, to live with Mother and me and take care of both of them.

If my schedule had been hectic before, now it was insane. Fortunately, my school work was behind me, but I had Mother and Aunt Muriel's legal affairs to attend to, boxes and boxes of papers to go through, half a dozen checkbooks to balance every month, countless tax forms to worry about, three heads of hair to wash and curl every week, three sets of groceries to buy, four eyes that needed cataract surgery, unending medical appointments, calls when I was at the office, and constant interruptions when I was home.

I soon learned that Aunt Muriel's dementia had released a mother lode of anger. We never knew what was going to set her off. Gracelita or I would fix her meals, and if she was in a bad mood or she thought there was something wrong with what we had served, she was not above picking up her tray and throwing it at us, food and all. Sometimes her weapon of choice was her own feces. There were major hygiene problems. Gracelita burned out a couple of times, and I did once, though we didn't let her see it. I remember the desperate feeling that I couldn't go on another day. People, not knowing the whole story, would ask me why I had taken on this responsibility, but I never gave it a second thought. Aunt Muriel had been the breadwinner when I was growing up, and she supported Mother, at least in part, for 60 years. I owed her a not insignificant debt.

Over the next three years she deteriorated steadily. The tantrums became fewer, and I began to empathize with her frustrations. Through no conscious effort on my part, a major shift began to take place inside me. My feelings of resentment dissolved as I imagined myself in her shoes. My heart went out to her, and we became very close.

She was terrified of being tricked into being put in a nursing home. She had done that to my grandmother Rosie, and she didn't want it to happen to her. I understood her fear, and I gave her my word that I would never do that. Together, we worked our way through one crisis after another. She started having falls because she was losing her balance. Once I came in and found her in a pool of blood, which turned out to be coming from her uterus—a not-uncommon event in elderly women, I later learned. I took her to the emergency room, and the gynecologist who saw her reported that she was fine, but he complained that he had had difficulty examining her because she was "virginal." Jokingly, I asked him:

"How many other 98-year-old virgins have you seen this week?"

It was a funny-because-I-was-uncomfortable joke. It was now clear that she had never had a serious loving relationship with a man. I felt sad for her.

Her accidents were becoming more frequent. In my mind, I was constantly balancing the risk to her safety against her loss of independence, which was so important to her. I began to plant the suggestion that she was getting too "tipsy" to be left alone. She finally consented to one last move.

I was able to get a bed for her at the same place where Mother had stayed. She was even looking forward to it. But when we arrived and got in the elevator, she looked around and said in a wistful voice:

"This is more institutional than I had imagined."

I wanted to cry.

She was miserable. She comforted herself with the belief that she was doing a psychological study of the patients and had to be "embedded" with them to observe their behavior. The reality was that they had her trussed up like a chicken. My heart broke all over again every time I visited her.

About three months later, on a cold day at the end of December 1989, I received a call from the nursing home at my office. She had died while eating lunch. Her heart had simply stopped. I went over and found her lying peacefully on her bed. I said good-bye. Then I met with the funeral director and signed some papers.

When I got home, Mother was sitting on the edge of her bed fully dressed, with her winter coat on and her bag packed. She looked up and me and said:

"My work is done now. You can take me to the hospital."

It was clear that she meant it. She was ready to die, too. Apparently she had been holding herself together with Scotch tape and string. I couldn't even begin to digest what she was saying. I had expected to have her for another six years. I had told her more than once that I was counting on that time, and I picked the number six because it was the difference in their ages. She was entitled to live at least as long as Aunt Muriel did. Also, we had gone through six years of major challenges, and we both deserved an equal reward. Teasingly, I reminded her that she owed me. She wasn't buying it.

I was still numb when we got in the car to take her to the Emergency Room. As I looked back, Sunshine was at the window watching, just as she had been when Sylvio was taken away.

They admitted her immediately. She was much sicker than I had understood. She hovered between life and death, consciousness and coma, for two weeks. I finally found the courage to tell her I would be able to manage if she decided to go, and a few minutes later she stopped breathing.

I scheduled a joint funeral for both of them in the same church where the service for Sylvio was held. Dallas officiated. People came from all over: Aunt Muriel's colleagues, Mother's friends, neighbors in the country who had known them both, and some of my friends who had never met them. Thanks to the help of my support group, there was a big reception afterwards at my house.

Then suddenly everyone was gone.

Gracelita moved out because I could no longer pay her salary and I needed to rent the apartment. Sunshine died a few months later. And there I was: my entire family had evaporated. My closest blood relatives were second cousins in Norway, and I had Sylvio's family in Brazil. But for all practical purposes, I was alone in my world.

Epilogue:

Redemption

A FTER SYLVIO, MOTHER, AUNT MURIEL, Gracelita, and Sunshine were gone, my life felt empty. Practically speaking, I had no family. I had fewer and fewer ties in Washington. Some relationships had drifted apart, a few friends had died, and many others had moved away. Even the support group had scattered. I had also lost interest in my job.

I was surrounded by the physical artifacts of my memories, and I realized that it was time to close this "museum" and move on.

Even Washington itself didn't feel right to me any more. My attitudes and beliefs had changed and I no longer fit in. My heart was already in California. Wherever I went, I seemed to be getting messages that it was time to fulfill my dream. I thought it was a "sign" when more than once I was told:

"You belong in California!"

Not only was I drawn to San Diego by the meditation garden, the friends I had there, and the openness of people in general, but I also had childhood memories of California. Mother, Aunt Muriel, and I lived in Berkeley when I was four. We had a rented one-bedroom A-frame cottage in Cragmont overlooking San Francisco Bay. My bed was in front of the bay window, and I had a world-class view of the bridge, the water, and the shore beyond. I was mesmerized by the lights as they came on at night, and I struggled to stay awake, not wanting to break the spell. I remember John Hinkel Park, woodsy glens, and high places where one could look out over the bay. It was an exciting and happy time for me, before things got complicated. Deep down, I had always wanted to go back. The view from the meditation garden evoked memories of Berkeley.

I had another tie to California as well. In the early 1900s, my grandmother's eldest sister Janet (pronounced JEN-et) left the family in Toronto, Canada, and moved to San Diego. In those days it was shameful for women to even take a job outside the home. She never returned, even for a visit. In fact, she scandalized the family when she became a Christian Scientist, and they cut her off. My mother was the only one who hadn't judged her and therefore remained her sole contact. I remember hearing about San Diego from her letters. As I thought about making my move nearly a century after she did, I felt as if I was following in her footsteps.

The challenge was to make it happen. By 1992, I figured that I could take early retirement and survive on my pension as long as I had some additional income from editing and translating. I retired officially in November and began to work at home. Among other assignments, I had a contract from my office to finish writing a manual that I had started years earlier. With regular meetings to incorporate feedback, the project became huge and ended up taking two years. California was never far from my mind.

The winter of 1993-1994 finally got me moving. In January, the city was pummeled with arctic ice storms and temperatures hovering below zero degrees Fahrenheit. It was too icy to go outside, even to put out the trash. The first time I did get out, I fell and hit my head on the ice. I didn't feel any pain because I was too angry.

"This isn't a way to live!" I told myself.

I came indoors and booked a flight to San Diego.

Once I arrived, in addition to seeing my friends, I looked at possible places to buy. I found the home of my dreams in Pacific Beach. It was a recently built condo/townhouse in almost-new condition, and the architecture inside was dramatic and beautiful. I decided to buy it, and I set the process in motion. Back in Washington, everywhere I went, I carried a copy of the floor plan, as if my dream might slip through the cracks if I didn't hold onto it. In February, I returned to San Diego to close escrow and find renters for the next six months. Then I went to work packing up and closing out my life in Washington, where I had lived since the age of seven. There were moments when I felt that I was embarking on a bold and scary adventure, but most of the time I was elated and filled with anticipation. My two black cats and I arrived on Halloween night, riding in on a Northwest Airlines transcontinental "broomstick."

California exceeded my expectations.

Starting a new life in my lovely townhouse not far from the ocean had me walking on air. Every experience was a thrill. I connected with the friends who had wanted me to come, and I made new friends quickly, especially people in the Arnold Patent network, my tribe.

In the weekly support group meetings, over and over I felt a wonderful rush of energy as the processes helped me release my attachment to troubling thoughts—which of course I still had on occasion, though they no longer engulfed me. Each time, I felt myself grow a little more. I discovered the joy of feeling my gratitude. As I delved deeper into this work, it became even more meaningful to me. Arnold had moved to Southern California shortly before I arrived. I attended many of his workshops and other events, including the annual five-day retreat at Asilomar on the Monterey Peninsula, and I got to know him personally.

I continued the alternative healing I had been doing in Washington, finding replacements for massage therapy and acupuncture, and later, homeopathy. I bought a chi-machine, which transports me to that realm of vastness where everything is equal and I am at one with the Universe. It is the most wonderful "high" I could possibly imagine. It has been my daily practice for 17 years.

The negative ions from the ocean helped to open up my breathing, and I was inspired to exercise and live a healthy lifestyle. Every day, I rode the entire perimeter of Mission Bay on my bike, stopping to lie on the beach when the weather was nice.

I traveled frequently and often worked at conferences back in Washington. My friends there told me that I looked twenty years younger. I started seeing men.

Despite my greatly improved condition, I still needed a doctor for my damaged lungs, and I found a very sweet man who espoused liberal causes and gave me wide latitude to experiment with alternative healing. Still, when he first learned that I had had breast cancer, he tried to get me to see an oncologist. I refused. We negotiated, and I ended up settling for a mammogram—my first in 18 years. Not surprisingly, it revealed scar tissue under the left nipple, where I had had my last surgery.

A few days later, a physician's assistant from a place called the Breast Center phoned and informed me casually:

"We're going to have to cut off your nipple so that we can examine it." She described the procedure.

I didn't take her proposal seriously for a single second. Not only did I think it was crazy to cut off my nipple, but I was certain that their studies would confirm what I already knew—namely, that there was nothing but scar tissue. I told her politely that it was out of the question, and that was the end of it. But afterwards, as I thought about what she had said, I resented the idea of others being so nonchalant about mutilating me with no strong evidence of cancer. I remembered how it felt to be a dehumanized object trapped in the "system."

Even if there had been something else besides the scars, I confirmed to myself once and for all that finding out was of no importance to me. Would I do anything about it? No. If I were younger, or if I had a family, I might feel differently, but in my circumstances, I wouldn't do anything different from what I was already doing for my health. Earlier, I had made this decision in the abstract, and now, facing a real choice only strengthened my resolve. It was totally clear to me: I would never consider mainstream treatment for breast cancer, and I therefore didn't need to expose myself to the discomfort and complications of a mammogram.

Over the years, California has opened me up in many ways. While at first I eagerly sought new teachers and new strategies, I gradually settled into a rhythm. More often than not, the lessons were experiential and I learned them more through my body than my head.

I have rarely been bothered by pain since the move. However, the problem in my hip came back for a brief visit about eight years ago. The onset was sudden: I pulled a muscle in exercise class. For about a week I couldn't walk. I didn't want to deal with doctors, so I decided to try a chiropractor—a resource that Nelson Hendler never mentioned in his book and is very popular in California. After a couple of weeks of adjustments, massage, and exercise, it went away. A similar trigger set it off again a couple of years later, and once again I was able to nip the pain in the bud.

Later, after a long sedentary period working in front of my computer, I got "kinked up" with pain in the neck and shoulder. Poking and pulling by the chiropractor revealed that the shoulder pain traced back to the same old spot on my spine, the L5. I saw him several times, had a massage, and did exercises, but the pain didn't budge. My heart sank: I was afraid that the old chronic pain was coming back.

Then I went for a regular appointment with my alternative doctor, Michael. He uses acupuncture, homeopathy, herbs, supplements, and other healing modalities. I told him about my pain and that I had been working with the chiropractor to get to the cause. Michael interrupted:

"But that's not the cause. The cause is deeper than that. The pain won't go away until you get to the real cause."

"I know that," I answered. "But it's complicated."

I was thinking of the many issues that I know I hide from myself. He interrupted:

"No it's not."

He silenced my chatter and needled me for about 20 minutes. No response. The sharp pain in my shoulder was still on fire. Then he made up a homeopathic formula using his own system. With one tiny pellet under my tongue, the pain disappeared in an instant.

Though it wasn't a permanent release, it was the same "pop," the same breakthrough, that I felt when Lorraine led me through Open Focus, and within a week the pain was gone for good.

Michael explained that the acupuncture had prepared me for the homeopathic remedy. The remedy was a resonance.[55] Resonance occurs when the remedy and the body are in perfect harmony—when everything is humming. It heals, he said, because it wakes up awareness. The opposite of resonance is dissonance, and it is caused by fear. We become afraid when we are separated from awareness and understanding. We are afraid of the unknown, and awareness dispels that fear. Using darkness as an example, he explained that it's not the dark itself we are afraid of, but the monsters that we imagine are lurking there. When we are separate and in pain, we are afraid of our monsters—the projections we cast on the unknown. The more we deny our fear and avoid opening up to look at it and see that it has no basis, the longer we stay in pain.

Of course! Carl Simonton had said the same thing in different words. So did many others. It was nothing new. But it was thanks to Michael, and the vividness of the lesson, that I finally got it. I remembered my old compulsion to get to the bottom of my diagnosis and pain, and I realized it had been fueled by a fear that could never be pinned down or conquered. The search for specific answers had only been a proxy. The real search was for *understanding*. With understanding, there are no monsters lurking in the dark. I am safe.

The teacher who gave me the greatest gift was Byron Katie.[56] Katie teaches self-inquiry and encourages her students, when dealing with a troubling thought, to ask themselves four basic questions. Discovering the answers to these questions becomes a journey that Katie calls "The Work." I was attending one of her intensive workshops, sitting in the front row so that I could feel Katie's calm and powerful presence. There were more than two hundred people in the room. We had already gone through a couple of days of long processes to release our attachment to the thoughts that haunted us. Now we had come to the really tough part. She asked us to think about the most horrible thing we had ever done. After giving us a few minutes to explore our thoughts, she called for a volunteer to come to the front. I knew it would take tremendous courage, but my gut was telling me it was time to give voice to my deepest guilt. I stood up and stepped to the center, shaking and crying. I finally gained enough composure to mumble the words:

"I had an abortion."

Katie asked the people in the audience to raise a hand if they or their partner had had an abortion, and hands went up all over the room. I realized I was doing the process for those people, too.

She then led me through her four questions. The last one was "Who would you be without that thought?" When we got to that point, I finally saw that there was an alternative to the guilt that had held me in its grip for so many years. As I finished, a wave of people came up and surrounded me with what might have been the biggest group hug in history. They *all* forgave me.

Not long afterwards, I woke up very early one morning and suddenly realized that I was being pulled out of my body. The next thing I knew, I was floating above it. The most wonderful sensation, like nothing I had ever felt before, enveloped me. I knew immediately that I was in the presence of my child. I felt her spirit surround me. I say *"her* spirit," because she was a girl now, though I had no doubt who she was. She said:

"Please don't worry. I'm fine. Be kind to yourself."

Then she left, and I gently returned to my body, still feeling her warm embrace. A few minutes later I felt an incredible surge of energy, a desire to leap over mountains, and it lasted for days.

I had long since forgiven myself for Sylvio's death and my grandfather's. With the forgiveness of others and the knowledge that guilt is my own fabrication, I was finally able to return my child's embrace and let go of my guilt.

Cancer and grief have been distant memories for a very long time. Questions remain unanswered: Did I ever have early metastasis in my spine? Was its progress halted with tamoxifen? Peter's megadoses of vitamin C? Deep relaxation, visualization, and biofeedback? Iscador? Homeopathy? Chinese medicine? Embracing cancer instead of fighting it? Building trust in myself? Gradually releasing my feelings of guilt? I'd like to think that each of these committed efforts helped to make me cancer-free, but of course I will never know. What I do know is that the journey was worth it.

My days now bring me countless moments of joy, and I am aware of a deeper bliss that is always there, even if I lose sight of it temporarily. I no longer seek out wise teachers and workshops and seminars. I use the resources I already have as new situations and new understandings come to me. My goal is to stay in the present moment. I try to live through my five senses and find rapture in everything I take in. Being with my senses keeps me in the present moment, which is always the best place to be—that place, according to Byron Katie,[57] where there's "nothing to do, nowhere to go, no one to be, no past or future, and everything feels right."

I am living my invincible summer.

Notes

(Endnotes)

Chapter 1

1. "In general, it is difficult to see a clear separation between normal functioning fibrous and glandular tissues and cancerous tissue, since their X-ray stopping powers are very similar" (http://lemur.cmp.uea. ac.uk/Research/mammores/mammography.htm).

Chapter 2

2. *What Women Should Know About the Breast Cancer Controversy* (New York: Macmillan, 1973).

3. In his memoir, *The Way It Was: 1907-1987* (Kent, Ohio: Kent State University Press, 1992, pp. 313-316), George Crile, Jr., wrote:

"I did my last radical mastectomy in 1955 and switched over to modified radical operation... but there were exceptions. A few years before, I had a patient, in her sixties, upon whom I had done an excisional biopsy of a small cancer in the upper outer quadrant of the breast. When I operated I did not know if it was benign or malignant and did not have permission to do anything more than a biopsy. To my horror, the lady stubbornly refused to listen to reason or to allow me to "complete the operation." I warned her of the perils and of the almost certainty of recurrences. That was what I had been taught. She promised to return if she ever had any further problem with her breast. She never did. I followed her for at least 15 years, and for the first half of the time I found it almost impossible to believe that she remained well....

"Suddenly after 50 years of complacent acceptance of radical mastectomy the surgical world is plunged in doubt...there is mounting evidence that simple mastectomy gives better results than the conventional operation... at present there is no basis for advocating any single type of operation for operable cancers of the breast...the challenge to the surgeon is to control the cancer as well as possible and to do so with the least possible harm.

"Soon it became obvious that there was going to be no significant difference in the survival...with the result that in 1957 all of us abandoned radical mastectomy..."

Around the same time, he wrote in *Life* magazine: "Those responsible for telling the public about cancer have chosen to use the weapon of fear. They have bred in a sensitive public a fear approaching hysteria. They have created a new disease, cancer phobia, a contagious disease that spread from mouth to ear...."

4. See: http://en.wikipedia.org/wiki/Rose_Kushner.
5. See: http://www.lightparty.com/Health/UnnecessaryMastectomies. html.
6. *Life*, March 1988.
7. In fact, Gilda died a year later, on May 20, 1989. She tells the story of her illness in her book, *It's Always Something* (New York: Simon and Schuster, 1989). See also: http://en.wikipedia.org/wiki/Gilda_ Radner.
8. World Health Organization, *Optimization of Radiotherapy: Report of a WHO Meeting of Investigators* (Geneva, 1980. Technical Report Series 644. p. 80).
9. The perfume was significant because Coco Chanel launched it on May 5, which she believed was a lucky day.

Chapter 5

10. Andrade, Margarette de, *Brazilian Cookery: Traditional and Modern* (Rutland, Vt., and Tokyo: Charles E. Tittle, 1965).
11. This problem came to a head in the 1980s as the settlement's population reached over 2 million, prompting major reforms that took care of the condition. See Vallarino, Roberto. Ciudad Nezahualcóyotl: Souls on the Run. In: Joseph, Gilbert M., & Henderson, Timothy J. (eds.), *The Mexico Reader: History, Culture, Politics* (Durham and London: Duke University Press, 2003. pp. 537-544).
12. See, for example, "The Baroque in Brazil," *Américas* special suppl. June-July 1974. 16 p; "The Ever-Brazilian Guignard," *Américas* 27 (5), 2-8, May 1975. Available at: www.murieltranslations.com/translations. html.
13. Mead, Margaret, and Muriel Whitbeck Brown. *The Wagon and the Star* (Chicago: Rand McNally, 1966).

Chapter 7

14. In *O Estado de Minas*, the daily newspaper of Belo Horizonte.

Chapter 9

15. The grandson of Inês married a Vasconcellos. Sylvio's family members in Brazil have traced their roots back to the 1700s, and the known

Mendes de Vasconcellos line descended from Inês goes through the 1500s. There is a gap of about 200 years.

Chapter 10

16. It was *Mycobacterium xenopi*. At the time, this organism was rare and there was only one case of it causing disseminated disease. Later it was found in patients with AIDS and other immunodeficiencies, but still it is not considered aggressive and not recognized as a cause of death. See: http://emedicine.medscape.com/article/223480-overview#a0104.

Chapter 11

17. Sylvio de Vasconcellos, *Crônicas do Exilo* (edited and printed in Brazil by Editora Líttera Maciel, Ltda., under the direction of Brasil Borges, 1979; rights reserved by Componential Publications, Inc., Washington, D.C.).
18. See: Carol Tavris, *Anger: the Misunderstood Emotion* (New York: Simon & Schuster, 1982).

Chapter 12

19. Text of his obituary in the *Journal of the American Medical Association* 113(14):1345, Sept. 30, 1939: "William Mortimer Brown: Rochester, N. Y.; University of the City of New York Medical Department, 1889; fellow of the American College of Surgeons; formerly on the staff of the Rochester General Hospital; past president of the Monroe County Medical Society; consultant in obstetrics and gynecology at the University of Rochester School of Medicine; aged 71; died, July 25, of illuminating gas poisoning, self administered."

Chapter 13

20. Reagan, Leslie J., *When Abortion Was a Crime: Women, Medicine, and the Law in the United States, 1867-1973* (University of California Press, 1998).

Chapter 14

21. "Bronchial washing: irrigation of the bronchi and bronchioles performed during bronchoscopy to cleanse the tubes and collect specimens for laboratory examination" (http://medical-dictionary. thefreedictionary.com/bronchial+washing).
22. The text of the report read as follows: "At this point the circulating nurse revealed that we were using sterile water for injection, and not saline. Therefore, the bronchoscopy of both sides, and washings were

repeated, after replacing the water with normal saline. The feeling was that the water may have led to lysis of the cells for cytology."

23. A later quote from the same report: "The esophagus was noted to have a thickened area in the posterior wall. . . . This was measured to be 17 cm down from the incisor teeth. A cup forceps, up-biting, held sideways, was used to biopsy this area, with care being taken to have a superficial biopsy of the mucosa, and not a deep biopsy which could potentially perforate the wall. A piece of tissue was removed."

24. World Health Organization, *op. cit.*, pp. 78 ff. Cited in Chapter 2.

Chapter 15

25. "When breast cancer has spread to distant organs, it is essentially incurable by present methods of treatment"—George Crile, Jr., *What Women Should Know About the Breast Cancer Controversy* (New York: Macmillan, 1973). Also: C.B. Mueller, "Breast cancer in 3,558 women: age is a significant determinant in the rate of dying and the causes of death"*Surgery* 83:123, 1978.

26. A tumor the size of mine may have been growing for at least 10 years. It probably doubled more than three times while I was waiting for a diagnosis (Michaelson, J., et al. "Estimates of Breast Cancer Growth Rate and Sojourn Time...,"*Journal of Women's Imaging* 1:11-19, 2003).

27. CEA stands for *carcinoembryonic antigen*. This blood test is considered especially indicative of colon cancer and was also used at the time to estimate cancerous activity in the breast, ovary, lung, rectum, and pancreas. However, its results can be affected by smoking, infections, or the presence of certain other diseases (hepatitis, peptic ulcer, COPD, inflammation of the gallbladder). It is not considered reliable for diagnosing disease. See: http://www.webmd.com/cancer/carcinoembryonic-antigen-cea. Better tests for breast cancer are available today.

28. The tomogram report read: "There is increased bony density involving the posterior aspect of the vertebral body at L5 on the right, as well as the adjacent pedicle, pars interarticularis and lamina on the right; also, a discrete well-defined area of increased density involving the upper right sacrum near one of the foramina."

29. Tamoxifen became commercially available in the mid-1970s, and doctors were still cautious about prescribing it. Later it became widely used, even as a preventive treatment for women at high risk for breast cancer.

Chapter 16

30. *On Death and Dying: What the Dying Have to Teach Doctors, Nurses, Clergy, and Their Own Families* (Routledge, 1969, 1973, etc.).
31. Quote from the architect Ludwig Mies van der Rohe, who had a strong influence on Sylvio's work. Mies is also famous for saying "God is in the details."

Chapter 18

32. Examples are the EMG (electromyograph), which measures muscle tension; the EDR (electrodermal response), for perspiration on the skin; the EEG (electroencephalograph), for electrical activity in the brain; the DST, for digital skin temperature; and the tensiometer, for blood pressure. The Center also had a small portable EMG that could be used for practice at home.
33. "Transcutaneous electrical nerve stimulation (TENS) . . . is the use of electric current produced by a device to stimulate the nerves for therapeutic purposes. [It] covers the complete range of transcutaneously applied currents used for nerve excitation although the term is often used with a more restrictive intent to describe the kind of pulses produced by portable stimulators used to treat pain." See http://en.wikipedia.org/wiki/Transcutaneous_electrical_nerve_stimulation. The technology was new and expensive, while today it is commonplace and cheap to buy. A salesman came to my house and had me sign a rental contract. My unit came in an elaborate fitted suitcase, and my monthly rental was more than what it costs to buy one today.

Chapter 20

34. O. Carl Simonton, Stephanie Matthews-Simonton, James L. Creighton, *Getting Well Again* (New York, etc.: Bantam Press, 1978; republished in 1992).
35. Jeanne Achterberg, Stephanie Simonton, O. Carl Simonton, *Stress, Psychological Factors, and Cancer: An Annotated Collection of Readings from the Professional Literature, with Bibliography* (Fort Worth, Tex.: New Medicine Press, ©1976). This study summarizes the research that had been done up until 1975 on stress and immunity, the effect of intense or chronic stress on cancer, the role of biofeedback, and *personality characteristics as predictors*, with a section that matches up psychological patterns with different types of malignancies. The book reviews 20 major articles on the subject, and the bibliography gives 170 titles from the medical literature, mostly from peer-reviewed journals.

Chapter 21

36. See http://www.openfocus.com, with books now available entitled *The Open-Focus Brain* and *Dissolving Pain*.

Chapter 22

37. Erhard Seminars Training, offered from 1971 until 1984.
38. See: http://en.wikipedia.org/wiki/Erhard_Seminars_Training.

Chapter 23

39. For example, Robert E. Griswold's Effective Learning Systems of Edina, Minnesota.
40. Monica Lewinsky shopped there in the 1990s. President Clinton was the alleged recipient of some of her purchases, including the racy novel *Vox*, by Nicholson Baker. Special prosecutor Kenneth Starr subpoenaed a record of her purchases, which triggered a court battle over First Amendment rights.
41. Nelson H. Hendler and Judith Alsofrom Fenton, *Coping with Chronic Pain: The Latest Treatments and Techniques for Dealing with It* (New York, NY: Clarkson N. Potter, 1979).

Chapter 24

42. According to Dr. Hendler's current LinkedIn page: "This clinic was listed in *Business Week* as one of the 8 best pain treatment centers in the United States ... Seventy-five percent of the patients came from 44 states and 8 foreign countries." The *Business Week* article and a photo of the mansion can be seen on the Internet. The LinkedIn entry goes on to say: "Dr. Hendler has written 3 books, 34 medical textbook chapters, and 56 medical articles." He is now based in California.
43. According to Dr. Hendler's Facebook, he took them from an elephant in Kenya in 1969. They weigh 133 and 89 pounds, respectively, and are cited in Rowland's Ward's *Records of Big Game*. A newspaper article on the sale of the house states, fittingly, that the man who built the mansion in 1900, Edward Burke, was "an original member of Teddy Roosevelt's Rough Riders."

Chapter 26

44. See: http://en.wikipedia.org/wiki/Anthroposophy.
45. See: http://en.wikipedia.org/wiki/Rudolf_Steiner.
46. See: http://en.wikipedia.org/wiki/Anthroposophical_medicine.
47. See: http://www.iscador.com/index.aspx. Placebo-controlled double-blind studies have shown than Iscador extends the life of

cancer patients and improves the quality of their life, but it has not been recognized as a cure by the general medical establishment. It is standard complementary care in Germany and Switzerland. For examples of these studies, see http://www.iscador.com/clinical-studies/index.aspx and numerous references on PubMed.

Chapter 27

48. Especially the work of Michael Halliday, as outlined in his "Notes on Transitivity and Theme in English," published serially in the *Journal of Linguistics* in 1967-1968. For further references, see: http://en.wikipedia.org/wiki/Michael_Halliday.
49. Vasconcellos, Muriel Habel, *Theme and Focus: Cross-Language Comparison via Translations from Extended Discourse* (Ph.D. dissertation, Georgetown University. Washington, D.C.: April 19, 1985).
50. See: http://www.murieltranslations.com/linguistics_mt_articles.html.
51. *Dictionary of International Biography: A Biographical Record of Contemporary Achievement*. vol. 11. Cambridge and London (England): Melrose Press, Ltd., 1975.
52. *Dictionary of International Biography: A Biographical Record of Contemporary Achievement* 21st ed. (Cambridge, Eng.: International Biographical Centre, 1990).

Chapter 28

53. Mace, Nancy L., and Peter V. Rabins, *The 36-Hour Day* (Baltimore and London: The Johns Hopkins University Press, 1981).
54. Some of his techniques resembled the Japanese style of acupuncture.
55. Michael explained that homeopathy works with the frequencies of the body's organs. When our organs are thriving, their frequencies resonate to create a whole being. When they are impaired, their frequencies weaken. The remedies, which are derived from plants and other forms of nature, have their own distinctive frequencies. The correct remedy will "wake up" the energy in the weakened tissue and help to bring it back to its natural frequency, thus bringing the whole body into fuller resonance.
56. See: http://en.wikipedia.org/wiki/Byron_Katie.
57. https://www.facebook.com/theworkofbyronkatie/posts/10150719085344150. April 29, 2012.